'*Though I Run through the*
triumph in the face of untl

      Becky Harling, international speaker and author

'Rarely will you read a more powerful telling of what it means to make your life a complete gift for others. Pamela Johnson tells the compelling true story of a Burmese family caught in the middle of wars, tribal conflict and hunger, and yet they choose to make their family's love, time, food and faith a complete gift on behalf of the hungry children who showed up at their doors. I was deeply challenged and humbled by this modern retelling of the miracle of Jesus feeding the 5,000 as God transforms a Burmese family's sacrificial gifts of love into a future of hope for many of Myanmar's most needy children.'

    Peter Howard, Chief International Operations Officer,
                                    Food for the Hungry

'Get prepared to be drawn in to this powerfully crafted documentary of one Christian Karen family's commitment to meet the needs of orphaned children in the context of a closed Buddhist nation under military rule and ethnic warring. Tears of empathy and compassion will be replaced by tears of hope as you see God's unbelievable sustenance of the Daw Gyi Daw Nge Orphanage that has served more than 1,000 children and teenagers. Will God call you to support this eternal work?'

    Dr Ruth Nelson, Professor of Psychology, Bethel University,
    Arden Hills, Minnesota; Co-editor of Religion, Disability,
                              and Interpersonal Violence

'What a gripping and well-researched story. This children's outreach in Myanmar is a story of faithful service and courage that will encourage your faith as you serve Christ today.'

Jon Hirst, Co-founder of Generous Mind

'Pamela Johnson has dug deep to tell the story of a Karen family in Burma with a remarkable legacy. Over three generations, this one family from the great-grandparents down, has taken in and cared for over a thousand orphans.

'It is easy to lose track of how many times they had to flee to save their lives from advancing armies. Yet their willingness to care for the neediest children never waned. Their story brings light to a difficult corner of the world, and shows how far God can use everyday people like you and me, if we are willing.'

Alan Pieratt, PhD, President of Children's Relief International

'This is a story that needed to be told and Pamela Johnson tells it well. She sets the story of one Karen family in its historical context, giving the reader a potted history of the country of Burma (now Myanmar) and a greater understanding of the extraordinary faith and love extended by this family to hundreds of children while at the same time struggling to survive themselves.

'Pamela clearly conveys the power of Christian love and example through generations and its ability to transform lives broken by war, poverty and neglect. At the same time, she paints a colourful picture of everyday life in Burma, with scenes of rocky crags, rice paddies and ox carts.

'A thoroughly interesting and inspiring read. Highly recommended.'

*Sheila Leech, Head of International Ministry at
Feba Radio UK and author*

'As president of Judson University and with our namesake being a major influence in Burma as well as to the Karen people, and since we continue that legacy by engaging Burmese-Americans, this book provides important context in three areas. It provides the reader with insights about contemporary history and culture in Myanmar. It provides an understanding of the varied experiences of the different people groups in Myanmar. It is a wonderful story of faithful obedience that both Christ followers and non-believers will resonate with for their own reasons.'

Dr Gene Crume, President, Judson University, Elgin, Illinois

'The news out of Myanmar (Burma) in recent years has been, at best, a mixed bag. After decades of a military dictatorship, famed human rights activist Aung San Suu Kyi took power as State Counsellor in 2010, a position akin to a prime minister. But her rule has disappointed many over her alleged inaction in response to the persecution of the Rohingya people in Rakhine State and refusal to accept that Myanmar's military has committed massacres. In addition, the nation has witnessed the unprecedented flight of over 700,000 Rohingya who have fled into Bangladesh.

'Amidst all the turmoil and pain, a compelling bright spot is the previously untold story of a Christian ministry that has brought solace, help and spiritual peace to so many. Pamela Johnson's book, *Though I Run through the Valley*, traces the heroic struggle of Daw Mya Shwe (who is also known by the more Western name of Emmerline Veronica) through civil war, forced relocation and military and guerrilla violence as she constantly opens her heart and life to orphans, abandoned children and others in need. The reader cannot help but be overwhelmed by her bravery and compassion in the face of extreme violence and human need. It is truly a story of Christian faithfulness that will grip any reader with sympathy for an oppressed people.'

Kenneth D. MacHarg, pastor, missionary, author

'I have had the pleasure of knowing Ms Emerald for over fifteen years. She is a precious lady, one of the modern-day heroes of the faith. I have witnessed her faith lived out as she continues to care for 150 orphans; she knows them by name and can tell you their story. She loves the children and they love her. When I met Ms Emerald, she told me, 'God brings them to my door, how can I turn them away?' 'I never married but God made me a mother to many kids.' Her story is one of faith and trust in Jesus Christ and will inspire you to trust God more and believe him to do great and mighty things.

'It's a joy to know Pam Johnson and to see her dedication and commitment to tell Ms Emerald's story with honesty and integrity. Thank you, Pamela, for a job well done! You are a true blessing!'

Patrick T. Klein, Founder and Director of Vision Beyond Borders

Though I Run through the Valley

A persecuted family rescues over a thousand children in Myanmar

Pamela Johnson

Authentic

First published 2020 by Authentic Media Limited,
PO Box 6326, Bletchley, Milton Keynes, MK1 9GG.
authenticmedia.co.uk

Royalties from the sale of this book will go to Vision Beyond Borders and
the Daw Gyi Daw Nge Orphanage.

British Library Cataloguing in Publication Data
A catalogue record for this book is available from the British Library.
ISBN: 978-1-78893-160-1
978-1-78893-161-8 (e-book)

Cover design by Vivian Hansen
Printed and bound by CPI Group (UK) Ltd, Croydon, CR0 4YY

This book is dedicated to my husband Phil and our children:
Ruth, Hannah, Joel, Sam, Ben and Abi.
Whether biological or adopted,
God has given us no greater earthly joy
than to call you family.

Since giving her heart to Christ in her teen years, **Pamela Johnson's** focus has been for the world's most vulnerable. Living out this passion, she and her husband, Phil, adopted three orphans from Korea and Vietnam to join their three biological children.

After raising their brood of six in Wyoming, the Johnsons spent several years in Dondo, Mozambique. With Children's Relief International, Phil oversaw the Green Door ministry which builds concrete block homes for the poor, while Pamela ministered to people dying of AIDS in a hospice called Project Life.

Hearing of the plight of the children in Myanmar, they responded to an invitation by Vision Beyond Borders to see the ministry, awakening them to yet another world of need. When not travelling overseas, Pamela and her husband live in Sierra Vista, Arizona with their dog, Punky.

Contents

Acknowledgements

Dr Tha Nyan (General Secretary/YMCA-Yangon): through the YMCA, you have become the voice of Christianity in Myanmar by serving in love everyone of all faiths. You actively live out 1 Corinthians 9:22 – I have a lot to learn. 'To the weak I became weak, to win the weak. I have become all things to all people so that by all possible means I might save some' (1 Cor. 9:22).

Naw Sandra Loo-Nee (Associate General Secretary/YMCA-Yangon): I have never seen anyone carry on two conversations simultaneously on two different phones before meeting you. In spite of your 24/7 job, you took the time to fly around with me in Myanmar to ensure the success of this story. You are an ambassador and representative of the indomitable Karen.

Ralph Kurtenbach: you were more than an expert in your field; you were an answer to my prayer in finding the right person to help me make sense of such an incredible story as Emmerline's. May God repay you for your patience, wisdom and kindness in the hours spent editing a fledging author's work.

Patrick Klein, Founder and Director of Vision Beyond Borders: your huge heart to take God's Word to creative access countries changes lives. Thank you for introducing me to the beautiful country of Myanmar and its wonderful and diverse people.

Ken MacHarg: your input was invaluable. Thank you for taking the time to answer questions about publishing and for a second pair of editing eyes on this book.

Renee Hanlin: thank you for believing this book could be written and for all the encouragement you offered along the way.

Patty Smith: more than lifting me up to Jesus in prayer and calling to check on the progress of the book – you accompanied me to Myanmar and spent hours playing with the orphanage children.

Prayer Warriors: Carole Allen, Jon Allen, Chris Bartman, Laura Bleak, Pat Elliott, Barb Elliott, Louise Garvin, Dee Hoffmann, Lou Kirkham, David Pool, Patty Rich, Maddi VanEpps and Kim Yount. You prayed, doing the work unseen by men but never ignored by our great God.

Most importantly, my husband, Phil. Our adventures together have taken us all over the world, and your homebody spirit never complains. How blessed I am!

Thank you, Lord, for allowing me a glimpse of your servants who are busy about your kingdom business, faithfully serving the least of these out of love and for your glory.

Preface

When I first heard about Emmerline, I didn't believe such a woman could exist.

'What? She is 86 years old and running an orphanage with 150 children in the centre of Myanmar?' I asked incredulously. 'How can she successfully manage this orphanage?'

I reflected on my own life. My husband and I live in one of the most affluent countries in the world and yet we discovered parenting is physically, mentally, spiritually and financially challenging. Having raised three older foreign-born adoptees, I understand the dynamics of taking in orphans who have suffered loss. Some days were glorious. Other days we just lived in survival mode and tried to figure out in which drawer to store our adopted children's emotional baggage because we couldn't figure out how to unpack it.

Then there was the day I sat down in the laundry room and cried because the stack of clothes was taller than I was, standing on my tiptoes. This scene spun around in my head as I considered the reality of caring for 150-plus children in an era void of the convenience that my Maytag washing machine had offered me.

Even more daunting than the physical challenges of raising adopted children were the bonding issues that often manifested themselves in a child's staunch independence. One day our oldest, Sam, took his younger siblings for a joy ride without considering that he was under-age, had no driver's licence and certainly had no permission from us to pursue his scheme. His mode of transportation was the old Chevy Citation that had been laid to rest in our driveway; for over a year it had been parked there unused. After banging on the carburettor a few times, he managed to start the engine. Not thinking that anything else on the car had worn out or failed, nor giving a thought to his whim, he and the other two took off down the street, smoke pouring out from underneath the bonnet. The old Citation quickly burst into flames as Sam drove it into a dry, grassy field behind a church. Thankfully, he had the where-withal to get the others out of the car before it was completely engulfed in flames.

As I pulled into our driveway, I had no idea why the fire trucks and an ambulance were whizzing past me towards the billowing smoke by our house. I didn't have to wonder long, as the authorities showed up at our door and informed us of our children's misadventures. It was one of many through the years that put us at our wits' end, causing us often to doubt our parental skills. Each of our adopted children had lived in orphanages before they came to their 'forever home', and all three had been impacted by their institutionalized lives. So, it was not without prejudice or curiosity that I questioned the success of this Karen children's home. Thus, when I heard the statement from Patrick Klein, the founder and director of Vision Beyond Borders, that a team was forming to go to Myanmar, I packed my bags. I joined the others for this trip in late 2017.

Upon arrival, our team travelled by plane north from the former capital city of Yangon to Taunggyi. Though we visited other wonderful places and ministered to the children in each one, my desire was to meet Emmerline and her wards. The day finally came when we arrived at her place, the Daw Gyi Daw Nge Orphanage and Old People's Home. The children were lined up at the entrance to greet us with warm smiles and giggles. I really had no preconceived ideas of what Emmerline would look like, whether she had a commanding personality or was fragile at her age. As it turned out, she was neither frail nor overbearing.

The children obviously love and respect this elderly woman. A blue silk, imprinted scarf draped her thin shoulders, matching the paler blue *longyi*[1] wrapped around her waist that flowed to her ankles. With dark hair swept into a chignon complementing the round glasses perched on her petite nose, Emmerline was strikingly elegant. She carried an air of dignity that one would expect from royalty, yet she was very humble and soft-spoken.

Emmerline's ethnic origin is half-Karen, half-Shan – a fact that plays a large part in her story. Her Burmese name is Daw Mya Shwe. Britain ruled Burma during her earlier years when she adopted the English name, Emmerline Veronica. We affectionately now call her 'Ms Emerald' because 'Mya' means 'emerald' in Burmese and she truly is a gem.

Emmerline welcomed me into the sitting room where the walls displayed portraits from a different era. In the faces staring back at us I could see a family resemblance. As she explained the relationship of each person, the history fascinated me. It was then that I made a commitment in my heart to learn how and why this extended family chose to raise over 1,000 children in a war-riddled country. It became apparent that this wasn't a matter of merely surviving in a country in continuous upheaval, but a family's history of thriving in spite of the hardships and leaving a legacy.

Getting the story took several trips back to Taunggyi. Her only surviving sister, Beatrice, who lives in Yangon, gave me valuable information from her perspective. I also spoke with the orphanage children, Emmerline's adopted son, Wingate, her daughter-in-law, Bella, and some of her friends. I immersed myself in the history of the country by reading books and articles and talking to different Burmese people. It all helped me to understand the dynamics behind the direction and decisions of the historical and current Burmese government. I did my best to be accurate on historical dates and facts, with the challenge that some have not been specifically recorded. A community's identity can have different spellings in an assortment of publications, all seeming to have authority. This comes with the translation of the word from one language to another or one alphabet system to another. I found it especially difficult to confirm the accuracy of a village name that was destroyed and no longer exists.

Myanmar (formerly Burma) has had a melting pot of eight major ethnic groups, 135 minor ethnic groups, 100 spoken languages, and over the years (besides the armed forces of the government) a number of insurgent armies.[2] It has been a minefield of disunity and disaster. When the country was riddled with bullets from assault rifles and rocket-propelled grenades from RPG launchers, many were running through the valley of death.[3] This family picked up just one weapon – the Bible. Their love for God and their love for each other spilled over into helping the most vulnerable among them.

They helped the underprivileged and orphans thrive. To thrive simply means to bloom or blossom. This definition has helped me overcome some of my prejudices about institutionalized living as I watched these happily adjusted children at the Daw Gyi Daw Nge Orphanage. They live there, even though over 70 per cent of them have one or two parents. Different reasons have placed them there. Their situation is not unique – in fact this scenario is true in the majority of children's homes in Myanmar.

The care of Myanmar's young is not without controversy, prompting a study in 2011 by UNICEF and the Department of Social Welfare. Results of this research were published in 'The Situation of Children in Residential Care Facilities in Myanmar'.[4] The report urged that children should be with their parents – a position I hold dear to my heart. In an ideal world, this should be the reality. Life in Myanmar has not been an ideal world for decades and I hope this story will bring to light some of the complications that prompted this Christian family to take in so many children and help them flourish.

Note: An asterisk will indicate a pseudonym for some of the children to protect their privacy.

Genealogical Chart of Emmerline's Family

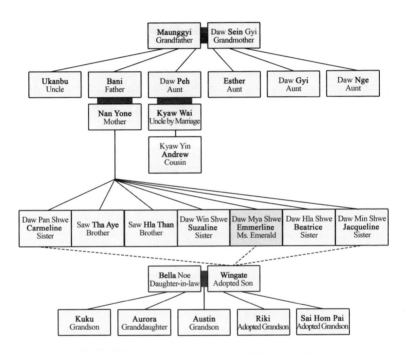

Daw Mya Shwe's family

The Burmese culture does not use a customary structure of surnames. Consequently, family relations can be difficult to remember and identify. It is also common when addressing a national to use honorifics (a title of respect). An example of this would be 'Daw' similar to 'Miss' or 'Mrs' in the English language. Many chose to adopt English names during the British

rule and used them interchangeably in identifying themselves –
adding to the confusion. The genealogical chart has been
drawn to help the reader understand the characters in relationship to Daw Mya Shwe (Emmerline). Though out of respect
the entire Burmese denominate should be used when addressing a national, for the sake of brevity and memory, only the
portion of a name highlighted on the genealogical chart will be
used in this book.

Pronunciations

Bamar (buh-ma)
Bani (**ba**-nee)
Bassein (**beh**-sayn)
Bennu (beh-**new**)
Bwe (bweh)
Chomden (**chom**-dan)
Daw Gyi Daw Nge Orphanage (daw jee daw nyai[r])
Daw Hla Shwe (daw **hlah** shway)
Daw Min Shwe (daw **min** shway)
Daw Mya Shwe (daw **m'yaa** shway)
Daw Pan Shwe (daw **pa**[r]**n** shway)
Daw Win Shwe (daw **win** shway)
Hla Than (hla tha[r]n)
Ho Pong (oo paw)
Hsa Pu Pey (saa **poo** pey)
Irrawaddy (aye-**ya**-wood-dee)
Jan Bahadur (jan ba-**ha**-du)
Kalaw (ka-**lo**[r])
Karen (ka-**rehn**)
Kayah (ka-**yah**)
Ke Ma Phyu (**ke** ma p-yew)
Kyat (chat)
Kyaw Nyunt (**jaw** n-**yoo**nt)
Kyaw Wai (jaw way)
Kyaw Yin (jaw yin)

Kyi Pyu Lake (chee p-yew lake)
Kywe (kway)
L.T. Ah Pon (ahh **po**)
Lahu (**lah**-oo)
Loi-Kaung (loy-kong)
Loikaw (loy-kaw)
Mai Shu (my shoo)
Maunggyi (Maw[n]-**jee)**
Mawchi (maw-**chee**)
May Pu (may poo)
Moulmein (mau-la-**myain**)
MuongNai (**mong**-nye)
Mya Zin (m'yaa sihn)
Myanmar (m'yaan-mah[r])
Nan Yone (nan **ywo**[n])
Pan Gway (pan gwayn)
Pa-O (pah-**oo**)
Papun (pa-**poo**[n])
Peh (pe)
Phayaphyu (pea-**ya**-pyew)
Pwo (poe)
Riki (**Ri**-kee)
Sai Hom Hpa (s-eye home pa)
Saopha (saw-bwa)
Saw Pweh Der (saw pway du)
Sein (sayn)
Sgaw (s-gaw)
Shway (sway)
Tachileik (taa-chee-**lake**)
Tatmadaw (**tat**-ma-daw)
Taunggyi (taw[n]**jee**)
Tha Aye (tha A)

Thada Mei Laung (tha-da **me** long)
Thay Doe Kwee (thay doh kwee)
Theramu (tha-**ra**-moo)
Toungoo (toung-**oo**)
Ukanbu (**oo**-kun-boo)
U Ne Win (oo nay win)
U Nu (oo noo)

These pronunciations were obtained with the help of five Burmese-speakers: Ku Gay Naypay, Shar Htut, Eh Klu, Nang Si Pin, Naw Ka Moe Eh and using the Voice of America's Pro•Nounce website: https://pronounce.voanews.com/browse-oneregion.php?region= burma (accessed 7 May 2020).

God's Protection in Taunggyi

For I am the LORD your God who takes hold of your
right hand and says to you, Do not fear; I will help you.
Isaiah 41:13

The sweat started to bead up on 9-year-old Emmerline's brow as she forcefully cut the potato and dropped it into the cooking pot. The sweet, earthy smell of the potato comforted her as she envisioned the meal that she would soon be eating with her favourite aunt, Esther, and her older brother, Hla Than. She liked her 14-year-old brother. He was talkative, easy-going and loved to make people laugh.

It was the hot season in Burma, and even though they lived in Taunggyi on a forested plateau of a 4,700 ft-high crag, the temperature began to soar uncomfortably. With more to worry about than the weather, Emmerline found a special camaraderie and reassurance in the presence of her aunt and brother. The rest of the family had made the 10-mile descent of over 3,000 feet by ox cart to Kyi Pyu Lake (White Crow Lake) to build a bamboo hut, should it become a necessary accommodation. They did this as a precautionary measure after the news media had informed the country in late 1941 that Burma had been drawn into the Second World War. Emmerline's family assumed it would be a long time before they were affected – or perhaps not at all if the British held their current positions or, better yet, pushed back the Japanese.

Nevertheless, her family and many others left this larger town sitting on the great rock, as it most likely would be targeted by the Japanese. Aunt Esther and her two charges would care for the house in Taunggyi until their future was more clearly defined.

Joining Emmerline in the work, Esther noted that the meal would be better with garlic and onions. She called over to Hla Than, handed him a couple of kyats[1] and instructed him to hurry.

Without hesitation, he jumped on his bicycle and rode towards the outdoor market, startling a jay that responded with a harsh squawking sound as it flew from its nest. In the slight breeze, Hla Than took in the sweetly intoxicating smell of the frangipani flower as he passed under the purple canopy of the jacaranda tree towering overhead. The normality of the day belied the truth that something else overhead would soon change their lives in a most formidable way.

The sudden, piercing sound of a warning siren and the deafening drone of incoming planes prompted Emmerline to instinctively drop her knife and run. It was the month of April in 1942 and the Imperial Japanese Army Air Service bombed Heho airport 300 miles directly north of Rangoon (currently named Yangon), the capital of Burma and just 24 miles from Taunggyi. Japan's quick advance surprised even the British. The Japanese were now within easy reach of the high plateau and just a few minutes away from their mission to destroy this strategic capital of the lower Shan State, where the British had administrative offices.

'Emmerline!' yelled Aunt Esther. 'Run to the shelter!' But Emmerline did not need to be told what to do. All school children had practised several times how to respond should they hear an air raid siren. Now reality met her disbelief as she tried to stifle her shock and fear. With trepidation, both Aunt Esther and her niece lifted the cover and jumped into the home-made bomb shelter. They were thankful that Aunt Nge had been insistent that they build a trench close to their grandmother's house where they lived. Seven feet deep, the shelter was covered with logs, zinc sheets and mud. Emmerline wondered if the shelter would be adequate protection from the terrorizing turmoil around them.

The smell of damp earth permeated the frightened girl's nostrils as she moved closer to her aunt. Her heart pounded so strongly that it pulsated in her ears. With a sick realization, Emmerline remembered that her older brother had gone to the market and had not returned. She couldn't help herself. She started to cry.

With no other option, Hla Than ran for the cover of a bridge when he saw the sky filling with unfamiliar planes and bombs starting to drop. Under the bridge he didn't just dodge debris and shrapnel from the exploding bombs, but also machine-gun bullets ricocheting around randomly from the low-flying planes. The Japanese were flying so close that he could see the silhouettes of pilots' faces. Blood splattered on him but he couldn't be sure whose it was. As structures started to go up in flames, the smell of the putrid black smoke nauseated him.

Hla Than's body began to shake uncontrollably with the sickening thought that he might not see his tightly-knit family again. His only option now was to wait under the bridge until the bombing subsided. He put his head down to protect it and to pray.

Below the crag in the village of Pan Gway by White Crow Lake, Uncle Ukanbu was diligently cutting bamboo to build a new shelter. He and his family had a clear, panoramic view of the skies above Taunggyi from White Crow Lake. As war planes flying over the plateau shattered the stillness, he watched in disbelief and with a sinking heart as the Japanese started to descend like a swarm of killer bees. His mother, Sein, had specifically asked him and his younger sisters to watch over the seven children of his dead brother, Bani. Now, with his sister facing imminent danger, two of Bani's children were in the midst of the carnage. Everyone in the village emerged and watched in horror as the sky filled with black smoke above the crag. Joining Ukanbu, the rest of the family knelt down and prayed earnestly, asking God to intervene on their behalf.

In one hour, hundreds of structures and lives were destroyed. Still shaking from shock, Hla Than watched the planes leave as quickly as they had come. Without hesitation, he left his bicycle where it lay under the bridge and ran as fast as he could, ducking and side-stepping a profusion of obstacles and injured people along the way. As he ran past the havoc, the only thing he wanted to see was his grandmother's house with his aunt and sister standing safely in front of it.

When the drone of the Japanese fleet had faded away, Emmerline nudged Aunt Esther. Slowly they peeked at the destruction from inside their home-made trench. They breathed a thankful prayer for God's protection, not only for their own lives, but for their grandmother's house. It was still standing, relatively untouched by the attack. The curious girl caught movement on the road and focused on someone running towards them.

'Hla Than!' yelled Emmerline. She couldn't remember a time when she was happier to see her brother. Unable to catch his breath and relieved to see them all alive, he collapsed in front of them. His skin was as white as the frangipani flower he had passed and his body trembled uncontrollably. Seeing his distress, Aunt Esther and Emmerline hurriedly filled a bucket with cold water and worked vigorously to cool him down. For the first time in a long time, Hla Than was without words.

Below the crag, Ukanbu saw the entire fleet of planes retreat from Taunggyi. He immediately hooked the Brahman cows to an ox cart and headed up the steep switchbacks to the plateau of Taunggyi. He had no idea what was waiting for him there – or, more importantly, who.

Eighty-five-year-old Sein heaved a tired sigh as she watched the dust from the ox cart trailing after Ukanbu. Many trials in the past had followed her and her husband, Maunggyi. They were from the Karen tribe, a people with a reputation of strength and independence. But this family's survival came not from their independence, but from their dependence on God. Whatever lay ahead, the biblical promise that trials produce perseverance and character[2] was the only comforting visionary truth at the moment.

2

Beginnings in the Irrawaddy Delta

*'For I know the plans I have for you,' declares the LORD,
'plans to prosper you and not to harm you, plans to give
you hope and a future.'*

Jeremiah 29:11

Trials and tribulations were a matter of course for Sein. Her
heart wasn't afraid to choose a difficult road; she took on her
family's battles and also those she waged on behalf of the children of Burma. Sandwiched between her tenacious temperament and toughness was a woman full of compassion and
action. This was the woman God used in southern Burma to
begin a legacy impacting the lives of over 1,000 children. Her
story was set in motion in the southern part of Burma with her
Karen tribe.

Some historians have concluded that Sein's ancestors
migrated through Tibet and China and arrived in Burma,
sometime after the Mon but before other ethnic groups.[1] The
Karen settled in south-eastern Burma and in the Irrawaddy
Delta.[2] Different Karen sub-groups exist such as the Sgaw,
Pa-O, Bwe and the tribe of Sein's family, the Pwo. By the mideighteenth century, the Karen felt oppressed by different ethnic
groups, especially the Burman (or Bamar, comprised mostly of

Theravada Buddhists). The Bamar consisted of two-thirds of Burma's population and was the dominant and ruling group.[3] The oppression birthed among the Karen a spirit of autonomy; and in the nineteenth century it swayed their acceptance of the British colonization.[4]

As the British expanded into Burma, economics, rather than religious drive, motivated them.[5] Unsympathetic to the Buddhist religion or the ruling Burman kings, the colonial rulers replaced the monarchy with their own administration. To gain control, the British selected ethnic minorities for positions of leadership, especially the Karen, who had been influenced by American missionaries.[6]

When the American Baptist missionaries had arrived in Burma in the early 1820s, the majority of the Karen tribes were animists. Surprisingly, the tribes were receptive to Christianity – more so than any other ethnic group. One theory explains this openness as influenced by a legend passed down that there was one Creator whose name was 'Y'wa.' One day a white man would bring a 'sacred book' and open up their understanding of him.[7] Consequently, when American missionaries shared the gospel, the Karen were open to receive it, and Christianity spread quickly among them. The first Karen converts, excited by their own personal spiritual transformation, were motivated to travel on extensive evangelistic trips sharing the gospel in their own language to their own people. The witness of one Karen to another was persuasive and successful.[8]

The missionaries then translated the New Testament, gospel documents and hymns into the Sgaw and Pwo dialects and built American Baptist Mission (ABM) schools. These schools taught the Bible to the Karen and also allowed them to receive a more diverse education (which included English language learning) than most Burmese schools offered. These qualifications gave the Karen preference by the British for employment in high positions. In time, though, this advantageous treatment ignited distrust from those who saw the Karen's desire for autonomy and their liaison with the British as an affront to Burmese nationalism.[9] This was the political pressure in Burma when Sein's first cry announced her arrival into the world in 1857.

Taught the Bible in the Irrawaddy Delta by the Baptists, Sein lived Christianity with her whole heart. The Bible's teachings on justice and mercy touched her soul and she experienced the transformation of the Holy Spirit. That change would carry on into this growing Christian's adult life.

Sein married into an agricultural family that was wealthier than most. Farming was hard work but the Karen tribes' skill at cultivating the fertile soil of the delta produced abundant crops. Houses were usually built on stilts to avoid flooding, constructed from bamboo and covered with thatched roofs. Sein's husband, Maunggyi, was a landowner with two rice paddies. Instead of a bamboo hut that would need to be replaced every two years, he constructed a home of quality timber. Though these two young adults were quite opposite in some personality traits, their marriage was as solid as their teak home.

In the Burmese Buddhist culture, a woman did not have the same freedoms as the men enjoyed. In the Karen culture, however, women were treated more equally and it allowed them to take active roles in decision-making within their families. Sein took advantage of this, never hesitating to speak her mind. Maunggyi was more easy-going than his wife. As Sein passionately expressed her thoughts, Maunggyi – whether he agreed with her or not – would often just nod and smile. The commonality between them, however, was their love for God, hard work and sacrifice. This combination of temperaments served them well as they raised their children.

Their first son, Ukanbu, arrived when Sein was in her early twenties. His birth awakened every maternal instinct within her. Later, another son, Bani, was born, followed by four daughters: Peh, Esther, Gyi and Nge. From Ukanbu's birth to the last child to enter their nest, the volume of mother's love from Sein grew greater than the waters of the Irrawaddy and Salween[10] rivers combined. Her vision for the success of her children, even if it meant sacrifice, was a priority. She was not one to keep her children at home to work and miss out on an education. Commonly, boys born into a farming community helped in the fields. But Maunggyi and Sein's children would go off to school, not to the rice fields nor kept behind for household chores. The decision to educate their offspring would be fortuitous and eventually carried a better return on their family's financial success.

When the children were of appropriate age, they were sent to Christian boarding institutions. The boys attended one of the ABM schools in Bassein[11] where they were taught English, Bible, maths, geography, history, health and practical industrial skills.[12] The girls attended an ABM school in Moulmein[13] further away from their home, but with studies designed for their scholastic success. By the time Ukanbu graduated from Standard 10 at the age of 15, a classmate informed him of a job in a small Buddhist village of 1,000 people in one of the Shan states in Burma. The opportunity for a job couldn't have come at a more needed time, as Maunggyi had lost his rice paddies.

The loss had its origins some ten years before Ukanbu was born. The Suez Canal opened in 1869, creating a connection between the Indian Ocean and Europe. A world of commercial opportunity lay before Burmese and other Asian farmers. As the canal was upgraded to handle more ships and increased travel, businessmen and farmers sought to supply the growing demand for goods. The opportunities to make money were not lost on the British colonial administration, which worked to increase Burma's rice cultivation. With pressure on the delta farmers to meet new rice demands, landowners borrowed money at high interest rates from moneylenders to farm more land to meet increased quotas.[14] When many landowners could not meet their financial obligations, they were foreclosed on and evicted, causing both landowner and farmer to lose their rice paddies. Maunggyi fell victim to this situation and lost his rice paddies to the moneylenders. Even in this difficult trial in their lives, God already had a plan for Maunggyi's family due north in Taunggyi.

At the end of the nineteenth century, the British colonial administration relocated their offices to Taunggyi, which then became the capital of the southern Shan states and a supply centre. At the same time, Sein's family left their home in the hands of extended family and boarded the train headed north to the cooler mountainous region, leaving behind the sultry delta.

Maunggyi – Emmerline's grandfather

Daw Sein Gyi – Emmerline's grandmother

Uncle Ukanbu

Daw Nge and Daw Gyi   Nan Yone – Emmerline's mother

Bani (front row, far left) and his soccer team

Back row, left to right: a cousin, Hla Than, Carmeline,
Grandmother Sein, Andrew, Tha Aye
Front row, left to right: Suzaline, Beatrice and Emmerline
(Jacqueline is not born)

Back row, left to right: Ei Ah Mar (Andrew's wife), Suzaline, Beatrice,
Hla Than, Jacqueline, Emmerline, Carmeline, Ni Ni, (Tha Aye's wife)
Front row, left to right: Andrew (Kyaw Yin), Nan Yone and Tha Aye

Left to right: Suzaline, Emmerline, Nan Yone, Carmeline,
Beatrice and Jacqueline

Wingate dancing (centre left)

Ox carts are still
used in Myanmar

Buddhist girls worshipping in
Yangon

Emmerline – Daw Mya Shwe

Daw Gyi Daw Nge
Orphanage – younger
children

Listening to a Bible story

Reading time in the orphanage

Playing a type of hopscotch

Washing floors in morning chores

Learning traditional weaving

Having a conversation with God

Older teens working
at the farm

Learning painting skills
while upgrading the
orphanage

So much to pray for . . .   . . . and be thankful

3

A Christian Family Among Buddhists

And without faith it is impossible to please God, because anyone who comes to him must believe that he exists and that he rewards those who earnestly seek him.
Hebrews 11:6

Bamboo huts and religious statues defined Taunggyi's landscape as White Crow Lake glistened in the valley nearby. The scents of the pine and eucalyptus trees welcomed the weary family of Sein as they travelled the last part of their journey by ox cart. Their exodus had not only left behind the stifling weather and rice paddies, but also their Karen family and friends. Now they would be living alongside the Shan people who were predominately followers of Buddhism.

The landscape would remind them daily of their contrasting faiths as the sun's rays reflected off the golden domed-shaped pagodas, glimmering unexpectedly like a neon light demanding attention. Though the two religions appear on the surface to have some similarity, at the core the two beliefs are quite contradictory to each other. Christianity extols one God in three persons: the Father, the Son (Jesus Christ), and the Holy Spirit, together known as the Holy Trinity. God the Creator is seen through the complexity of his creation and revealed in the

Bible by forty historical writers covering a time period of 4,000 years. These writers documented over 300 fulfilled prophecies of his Son, Jesus Christ the Messiah, in order to declare God's purpose in the affairs of humanity.[1]

Buddhism does not base its belief on any deity, but instead upon the meditations of a man named Siddhartha Gautama. There exists no official record of his birth or death during the era attributed to his lifetime. Some historians doubt his existence, while others feel many of his life stories are legends. Buddhist religion is based on Siddhartha Gautama's precepts rather than the authenticity of his actual existence among his followers.[2] The earliest story reveals that Siddhartha Gautama was initially shielded from suffering in his youth by an overly protective father. Then when he stepped out into the real world, he was confronted with the reality of old age, illness and death. Overcome by these tragedies, he went on a pilgrimage to seek answers, determined to find the solution to all suffering. In the process of this spiritual journey, he attained 'Nirvana' or 'Enlightenment' and became known as the Buddha ('The Enlightened One'). In four Noble Truths, he taught what the cause of suffering is and how to end it.[3]

The first Noble Truth is that humankind has selfish needs that are not always met. Even when they are, it is a temporal state, leaving a person's heart empty. The second Noble Truth expands upon the first: lustful craving is the centre of all evil and it comes in three forms: covetousness, misconceptions and hostility. The third Noble Truth admonishes Buddha's followers to extinguish selfish longings and reach Nirvana (a supernatural state devoid of self-awareness and thus a relief from anything that would cause suffering). The fourth Noble Truth explains how that is done via a list of principles called the 'Eightfold Path'. Some of the principles are comparable to the Ten Commandments of the Bible's Old Testament. However, Buddhism emphasizes that people must cultivate control over their own mental and emotional state in order to live out these rules.[4] As a belief system, Buddhism does not place trust in any outside source for a person's inner spiritual strength, unlike a Christian's dependence on God, which is central to Christianity.

The Bible explains that God placed humankind on earth, to call people into a relationship with the Trinity. God is holy, and any relationship with him must be pure. God gave humanity a set of commandments to follow, which was broken, unveiling hearts incapable of the pure love or power necessary to follow God's laws. Humanity's sin formed an abyss of separation from God, resulting in suffering and death. But God, who knew people were neither capable of living without sin nor living independently from him, had a plan of restoration before humanity was ever created. The Bible explains that all sin and deserve death.[5] But God miraculously united justice and mercy. He chose his Son, Jesus, to be born as a man to take the punishment for sin.[6]

This sacrifice became the bridge over the abyss to bring back anyone who accepts that they are in need of a Saviour who can restore their relationship with God.[7] Jesus came back to life demonstrating God's power over death and his will to restore all things. The Holy Spirit's presence in the heart of a Christian transforms their heart to worship and love God and to love others in purity.

In their pagodas, Buddhists also worship and bow down. They do so at golden statues of Buddha as a means of humbling themselves while they recite his precepts and honour his memory with offerings of food, flowers and money.[8] They deeply love their founder as the Enlightened One who showed the pathway to Nirvana. It is a difficult and lonely fight to self-denial as they strive to control their eternal destination. In spite of this heavy cost, a Buddhist has no guarantee that enlightenment will ever occur.[9] On the other hand, Christianity teaches that salvation through Jesus is both free and secure.

At his death, the spirit of the person who receives the free gift of salvation through Jesus Christ is ushered into God's presence; one day they will receive an eternal body and everlasting life in heaven with the Trinity. People who have not been restored to God through repentance spend eternity separated from God and in perpetual suffering.[10]

In this religious tension, the family of Sein settled among the Shans. They viewed as inevitable that their business and lives would interact continually with the Buddhists. Ukanbu accepted a job in a government office, prompting them to move from the delta. Within five years of their arrival, he advanced to being a chief administrator for a Buddhist Shan prince.

In the pre-colonial period before the arrival of the British, the Shan states were mostly autonomous, paying tribute to the king of Burma. Once the British took control, these states were under the rule of individual *saophas* (rulers or princes) as feudatory princely states of the British Crown, and Taunggyi was inaugurated as the capital of the southern Shan states. These *saophas* had immense responsibilities and were hard workers who cared deeply for the welfare of their people. They oversaw very wide areas in their jurisdiction and consequently needed a number of servants. They would often make their way to Taunggyi for meetings and conferences where many of them lived in palaces – their own home away from home. Ukanbu, as an employee of the Shan prince, met a friend and advocate in an American doctor who had moved to the area.

Dr A.H. Henderson, a missionary to Burma, worked with the ABM. He had relocated from MuongNai to Taunggyi after his wife almost died from Blackwater Fever.[11] Henderson's work in MuongNai proved to be a high-risk area for mosquito-borne diseases. The high elevation of Taunggyi offered a respite from the valleys that attracted these menacing and dipterous insects. After all, he had visited Taunggyi once a month from MuongNai and was very familiar with the local Christians, Sein and Ukanbu in particular.

Sein worked alongside Henderson, holding his medical chest with pride and assisting him in his visits to the sick, lonely, shut-ins, single mothers, widows and orphans. This new 'nurse' developed hands-on skills, not only caring for children but also acting as a midwife for expectant mothers. One family moved to Taunggyi with their two youngsters and birthed eighteen more children. It became an annual event for Sein to stay at this couple's home for three or four days, supervising and assisting each birth.

Henderson also had a desire for the Buddhists and *saophas* to hear the gospel. He openly shared his faith as he diligently used his medical skills to save lives. Christian doctors in Burma had many opportunities to demonstrate compassion and care, which opened doors for conversation about life and death and the great divide between the two. As Ukanbu and Henderson conversed with the Shan prince, their desire was for him and the people of Taunggyi to be introduced to the love of God.

But Sein's ministry would not just be with Dr Henderson and the Shan. This industrious mother joined three other Christian women to minister among the Pa-O tribe. This quartet would visit different villages sharing the gospel through Bible reading, singing, teaching, preaching, and giving money to those in need. Sein's energy knew no bounds as those who responded favourably towards her were blessed by her love. Soon, this un-relenting dedication and desire to help others would be spent on the hurting children of Burma.

The forested hills close by provided ample teak for Maunggyi and Sein to build a large two-storey home among the other modest bamboo huts on the plateau. What may have appeared to their Buddhist neighbours as extravagant and expensive, was an indispensable asset for God's call on this family. The spaciousness would not be wasted when in 1905 news arrived about a village in Kayah State, the eastern part of Burma. Hearing it would send Sein on an urgent errand away from Taunggyi.

4

The Children and Grandchildren of Sein

Whoever welcomes one of these little children in my name welcomes me; and whoever welcomes me does not welcome me but the one who sent me.

Mark 9:37

Word came to Sein that a forest fire had burned down a large village of bamboo and thatched-roof huts in the neighbouring state of Kayah, home of the Karenni tribe. The fire bore down on the helpless village so quickly that many villagers lost all their possessions – others lost their lives. This Karen mother, who was in her late forties at the time, didn't hesitate to ask permission from Maunggyi to go to the Karenni tribe to help alleviate some of its anguish.

With her husband's blessing, Sein loaded an ox cart and headed south for Kayah State to see what she could do to help. When she arrived and discovered eight boys had been orphaned, she returned home with them and a resolve to raise them as her own.

Even before these orphans had settled in Taunggyi, Sein was opening her doors again. From friends in the Irrawaddy Delta, she received news of more children in a crisis situation.

A stepmother had tried to poison two of her husband's boys, not wanting anything to do with children not her own. Sadly, a similar situation happened in another blended family in which a stepfather was caught unmercifully torturing his two stepsons.

Another son lost one parent, while the remaining parent, unwilling to take the responsibility, abandoned him. Poverty is often one of the underlying factors contributing to such dysfunctional behaviour. With no hesitation in her heart, Sein travelled by train, boat and ox cart, soon finding herself back in the delta taking in these five needy boys. This Karen couple's decision to bring thirteen boys into their home was soon to birth a new way of life for the entire family.

The relative political peace of the British colonization allowed the family to reap the fruit of their labours and have ample material blessings to share with others. The assets Maunggyi had brought from the delta and Ukanbu's prestigious job supplied the basic needs. To meet the children's appetites, their table was laden with the cultural and culinary choices of sticky rice with banana leaves, eggs, squash, calabash, tomatoes, potatoes, tea, fermented fish paste, mangoes, papayas and oranges. To meet the need of the children's growing minds, Sein had definite plans.

The family arranged for the new boys' schooling at the ABM in Taunggyi, not accepting anything less for their education than they gave to their own biological brood. Most important, though, was their spiritual needs. After all, these orphaned boys entered a home whose foundation was set on Christian principles.

Maunggyi spent many hours studying the Scriptures and diligently teaching his children its treasures. He took seriously the commandment on Sabbath rest and on Sundays did not allow anyone in the family to engage in outside activities except church attendance. He believed that all the children should be well-educated and develop the talents that God had bestowed on them, whether in leadership, music or service. His wife consistently disciplined any child in her home to be an exhibition of proper etiquette and manners. All these rules and regulations could have been overbearing had it not been balanced by Maunggyi and Sein's love and nurturing.

Special family times of playing, praying and singing brought the family together, with plenty of time for this closeness on Sundays. This routine bore benefits. The melodious and meaningful hymns they sang unified the children not only in spirit, but strengthened the truths learned. This faith would need to be strong, for more children would be arriving on the family's doorstep, but in an unforeseen way.

Sein was happy and proud of her second oldest son, Bani, when he came home with the announcement that he too had found employment in Taunggyi. He, like Esther, had a biblical name – albeit more obscure – not just a Burmese or Karen name. This fact emphasized that to their parents, the family's Christianity was more important than ethnicity. Bani was more outgoing than his older brother, Ukanbu, whose quieter countenance was more like that of Maunggyi. Though he was shorter than his sibling, Bani's stockier athletic frame gave him an advantage in the municipal soccer team he played in when he would compete against Ukanbu's Shan State administration team. The family loved to watch the two play in these local games that were celebrated with bagpipes and drums. Bani's outgoing personality was a good fit for his new job overseeing bazaars in Taunggyi.

Villagers arrived from all over the area to sell goods at the marketplace. Some balanced baskets of wares on their heads;

others had piled ox carts high with oranges, bananas, tea, chillies, woven baskets, medicine or whatever they had brought to sell. These bazaars happened every five days and were as much a social event as they were a means to earn money. Baptist evangelists took the opportunity to set up a meeting place and preach the gospel in the bazaar, selling their tracts and Scriptures. Bani and his younger sisters, Gyi and Nge, were a part of this effective method to reach many who had never heard the gospel.

A compassionate man, Bani graced the halls of a hospital or police station if he thought someone needed comfort and prayer. His volunteer position as a leader for Christian Endeavour[1] – a programme for children between the ages of 4 and 12 – created a venue for his singing voice to shine. He and the children performed at funerals and were a common sight during the Christmas holidays. With lanterns in hand, the merry crew visited neighbourhoods singing their favourite Christmas carols. Bani's life was more than full on the day a young lady in the bazaar caught his eye.

The girl, Nan Yone, had been working at home and helping her family for years. Her mother had passed away when Nan Yone was very young. Like so many other girls, she left school after Standard 4 to help her family by selling her father's produce in the market. Food on the table was a higher priority than paying school fees and buying uniforms. Though the British raised the educational expectations and encouraged girls like Nan Yone to stay in school, she had no choice but to be satisfied with her level of education. Her father, an employee of the British government farms, was intimidating, with tattoos covering his entire body. Tattooing oneself was a common spiritual practice of the Shan for protection and prosperity.

Neither the father nor Nan Yone herself objected to Bani's interest in her. Bani had decided that he would *not* remain a bachelor, though this was going to be the destiny of his older brother, Ukanbu. The slender and shy young Nan Yone won his heart. Now he wondered what the reception would be when he announced to his family his intention to marry her.

Marrying at age 16 was common for girls in Burma. Bani knew it wasn't because Nan Yone was young that his family might object. It wasn't because she was not humble or didn't show respect to him that might cause concern within his family. After all, she had proven herself submissive within her childhood family. From the earliest light until late at night, hers was a life of home chores that fell on Shan women. It wasn't any of these possible scenarios. The issue was that Nan Yone was a Buddhist about to marry into a very stalwart Karen Christian family.

Nevertheless, this interfaith couple married, a choice that did not fall on blind eyes, especially those of Bani's younger sisters, Gyi and Nge. In them an undercurrent of resentment against Nan Yone began. They determined that they would rather not marry at all than marry the wrong person.

Nan Yone and Bani embraced married life and settled into raising a family. The first grandchild arrived for Maunggyi and Sein when Nan Yone gave birth to Daw Pan Shwe in 1922. She was the first of seven children born to the couple in a span of thirteen years. When she was older, their first child gave herself the English name Carmeline Candice. Naming oneself was common practice for school-age children during the British era in Burma. Gifted, bright and responsible, she was a sketch of the stereotype of an oldest child. A son, Tha Aye, came bouncing into the world after Carmeline with a love for the outdoors – a perfect match for the older men in the family who loved soccer. Bani and Nan Yone had been blessed with a girl and boy, but they were not the only couple birthing grandchildren.

Peh, always the one to help her mother with the chores, presently had her own family to care for and welcomed a son, Kyaw Yin. Given the biblical and common English name of Andrew, the boy had a sensitive and easy-going personality like his mother. However, unlike his cousins, he decided that his studies were a chore and a bore. His hands usually held a violin or soccer ball rather than a textbook. Andrew would be his mother's first and last child, but not so for Nan Yone, who was about to birth her second son.

Perhaps Hla Than's place in the birth order factored in his need to be heard, as he loved to constantly talk. His emerging loquacious personality was accompanied by a humorous side upon discovering his joy at hearing people laugh, especially his siblings. He was the last of the grandsons to be born.

Daw Win Shwe's birth broke the pattern of boys and gave Carmeline a sister. In her school years she became known as Suzaline Phyllis. Suzaline was rumoured to be more beautiful and was a bit plumper than her sisters.

For most people, four children would be a full house, but not for Bani and his wife. Daw Mya Shwe (Emmerline Veronica) joined this expanding household. Emmerline was a strong child with a reputation for being fearless – a valuable attribute in the years ahead. She would be the one called by God to carry on the family's legacy of doing more than giving 'a cup of cold water'[2] to the children of Burma. Daw Hla Shwe, or Benadine Beatrice as she called herself in English, was second to last to be born. Her Burmese name was more fitting, declaring her inner beauty. 'Hla' in Burmese means 'she/he who is beautiful' and her beauty would prove not to be merely in appearance, but in her sweet nature.

In 1937, though unknown to Bani and Nan Yone at the time, their last daughter would arrive – Daw Min Shwe or Jacqueline Allison. Perhaps more children would have been born in the years after Jacqueline's birth, but neither Bani nor Nan Yone foresaw the tragedy that would fall on them on the forty-fifth day after the baby's presentation.

Bani became suddenly ill with a fever and abdominal pain – symptoms mimicking typhoid. But the sickness was not typhoid and the medical professionals had no idea how to treat him. Use of broad-spectrum antibiotics was not an option and the available doctors didn't have the equipment to run sophisticated tests. As Bani's health declined rapidly, he had to accept that his time with his family had come to an earthly end.

The sorrow of leaving his wife and children was overwhelming. However, the thought of his dear wife spending an eternity in hell terrified him more than leaving her. With an urgent voice, Bani asked Nan Yone once again to leave her Buddhism and consider the teachings of Christ. His bereaved spouse listened respectfully, clutching her crying newborn to her breast. Her deeply-rooted belief in Buddhism had a hold on her tongue, even in the presence of her dying husband. So, Nan Yone remained silent.

Though hard to understand and equally hard to accept his impending death, his faith in God would not waver. Now more than ever, Bani wanted to minister to his family, his friends and the municipal officials as they watched helplessly at his bedside while his strength ebbed away. Slowly, with as much clarity as Bani could muster, he softly sang all five stanzas of 'Abide with Me' while everyone listened, too overcome to join in.

Abide with me; fast falls the eventide;
The darkness deepens; Lord, with me abide;
When other helpers fail and comforts flee,

Help of the helpless, oh, abide with me.

Swift to its close ebbs out life's little day;
Earth's joys grow dim, its glories pass away;
Change and decay in all around I see –
O Thou who changest not, abide with me.

I need Thy presence every passing hour;
What but Thy grace can foil the tempter's pow'r?
Who, like Thyself, my guide and stay can be?
Through cloud and sunshine, Lord, abide with me.

I fear no foe, with Thee at hand to bless;
Ills have no weight, and tears no bitterness;
Where is death's sting? Where, grave, thy victory?
I triumph still, if Thou abide with me.

Hold Thou Thy cross before my closing eyes;
Shine through the gloom and point me to the skies;
Heav'n's morning breaks, and earth's vain shadows flee;
In life, in death, O Lord, abide with me.[3]

Bani closed his eyes and drew his last breath, believing God, who never changes, would care for this burgeoning and vulnerable family.

5

Growing Up Among Extended Family

So do not fear, for I am with you; do not be dismayed,
for I am your God. I will strengthen you and help you;
I will uphold you with my righteous right hand.
                                        Isaiah 41:10

The prospect of Nan Yone's widowhood, as a young mother of not one or two children but seven under the age of 14, was overwhelming. She had never felt so alone. Not that Bani's sisters, Gyi and Nge, were outwardly unkind to her, but they made it obvious that they did not approve of her religion nor her limited education. And that didn't begin to mention whatever they may have thought of her ethnicity as a Shan. She had never felt their equal and had gladly hidden under the protective wings of her husband, who was no longer her advocate. She wondered how she could possibly care for the children whom she concluded fate had bequeathed her, with no prospective means to support them.

Nan Yone questioned what she had done to provoke this sorrow. Had karma played a role in this, as Buddhism had taught her to believe? Do actions in a former existence control one's fate for good or evil in one's present life? When stress came in violent waves threatening to drown Nan Yone's sanity, she lost her breast milk for baby Jacqueline.

Bani's mother, Sein, was glad that Maunggyi, who had been dead for five years, had not lived long enough to bear the sorrow of his son's death. Now, at 80, she knew she was too old to be responsible for more children. The thirteen boys she had originally raised from Kayah and the delta had grown up and were thriving, as were many other children who had come to live with her charitable household. Those who had been blessed with higher aptitudes graduated from high school and became army officers, lawyers and medical advisors. Others had become teachers, compounders (one who attends wounds and dispenses drugs) and clerks. She was thankful for their successes.

Turning away a child in need of a mother, food and schooling was not within her Christian character. Her home had been a constant ebb and flow of children coming and going. Sein managed because Ukanbu, Esther, Gyi and Nge had returned to offer help after they had graduated from school. After all the years of caring for other children, she wasn't about to see her grandchildren abandoned. She knew exactly who could come alongside Nan Yone and raise Bani's children.

When asked, the four siblings wholeheartedly embraced the idea. The bachelor uncle and his three younger spinster sisters took over the care of their nieces and nephews. Ukanbu became so much the father figure that Beatrice thought he was her father until she learned that he was actually her uncle. Jacqueline would only know what relatives described of her father. Bani was always a man of her imagination.

Their enthusiasm to raise the children well translated into a lot of do's, don'ts and discipline, as the model had been chiselled for Uncle Ukanbu and his siblings. As schoolteachers, Aunt

Gyi and Aunt Nge carefully taught the correct manners and acceptable behaviour befitting their Karen culture as the family lived out their Christianity within the colonial British rule.

Though Aunt Nge was known for her thoughtfulness and wisdom, her strong personality commanded respect, at times striking fear in Emmerline's heart. The intimidated niece closely guarded the secrets of her soul around the strict aunt. Instead Emmerline went to Aunt Esther, who was equally as sweet in demeanour as Aunt Nge was stern. The kinder, gentler aunt was able to provide a great listening ear and a tender heart whenever Emmerline needed her.

Thankfully, their home was not defined by all the rules and discipline. The aunts and uncles loved Bani's children and the children loved them. Many hours of laughter and music reverberated within the walls of the sitting room. Aunt Nge's proficiency in violin, guitar and piano enabled her to teach violin and piano to Carmeline, the violin to Andrew, and the piano and organ to Suzaline. Emmerline mastered the mandolin and tinkered on the piano and guitar. The other children living with them at the time did their best, playing the banjoline or ukulele.

All the children learned to perform in harmony by gathering in the sitting room to spend time singing hymns along with English songs learned from the British, Americans or other children at school. Some favourites were: 'Moonlight on the Colorado' (Robert King/Billy Moll/Barbelle), 'Somewhere in Old Wyoming' (Riley Puckett), and 'Carolina Moon' (Burke & Davis). With a very sweet voice by the age of 4, Jacqueline would sing her favourite song when given the chance: 'Over the Rainbow' from *The Wizard of Oz*. The song captured the imagination of young Karen girls in Burma who wanted to be whisked away to a magical place, much like the character

Dorothy – a place where hope is unending, and problems don't touch their lives.

Among the repertoire of hymns they loved to sing were, 'What a Friend We Have in Jesus' (Joseph Scriven/Charles Crozat Converse), 'Sweet Hour of Prayer' (W.W. Walford), 'Under His Wings' (Cushing/Sankey) and 'Jesus, Still Lead On' (Nikolaus Ludwig Von Zinzendorf).

Nan Yone was often part of these gatherings. Tha Aye's rich and strong voice triggered her memory of Bani and his singing on their last day together. Since her husband's death, her contribution to the family was that of servitude. Her sisters-in-law, both talented and educated, could provide special training to enhance the children's education. She had found her own place by serving her children and in-laws with the menial tasks that accompany a large household – knowledge well-cultivated from her childhood.

Nan Yone didn't mind. Life had settled down from five years ago into a sense of ordinary, and for that she was grateful. At family outings, whether for soccer, picnics or swimming, this single mum saw glimpses of Bani in her children's faces. It stirred in her a perplexing mix of pain and pleasure. Except for their father, the children had everything they could possibly need. Like the sun peeking out from a heavy cloud after a rainy day and forming a rainbow, she laid bare a belief within her that their future might get brighter. But the golden era of the British rule was about to end.

As 1942 was beginning, the clouds accumulating on the Burmese horizon were neither light nor dissipating but were, in fact, clouds of war, as dark as evil and quickly gathering strength. Word had reached Taunggyi that the Japanese were pushing back the British in lower Burma. Sein's family needed to be prepared.

6

Finding Refuge in the Japanese Occupation

But the Lord is faithful, and he will strengthen you and protect you from the evil one.

2 Thessalonians 3:3

In the face of what might come, the family moved below Taunggyi to White Crow Lake leaving behind only Esther, Hla Than and Emmerline to temporarily attend the house. The rest tried to establish a semblance of normality by building a shelter in their new refuge. But for Beatrice, it began a new nightmare.

The 7-year-old woke up one day feeling woozy as the pain in her head caused her to roll over to a better position on the floor. She couldn't remember ever feeling this poorly and she was too tired to do much else but lie there.

Her symptoms pointed to malaria, as the lower elevation and their proximity to White Crow Lake made the mosquito-borne disease a threat. Her flu-like symptoms and rising fever were not improving, and worse, pustules began to erupt on her skin – a sign she had contracted the dreaded and deadly smallpox virus. The disease advanced like an army of soldiers within Beatrice's body for a few days, potentially exposing everyone around her. This young girl was ill and frightened. Beatrice's nature usually made her a protector, not the protected. Though older, Emmerline had often been the beneficiary of her sister's care.

During an earlier time, Emmerline and Beatrice were on their way to church. Together they decided that fishing in a local stream would be a day better spent. Thinking their plan was airtight, their absence was discovered nonetheless by Aunt Esther. When confronted, Beatrice took the entire blame to keep her sister from getting into trouble.

No longer feeling brave, Beatrice's underlying fear – for herself, her family and her country, where children were no longer safe – was intensified by her sickness. A kind pastor from the village, U Poe Tun, spent time with her and her family because of the uncertainty of what lay ahead. Even though Beatrice was young, her circumstances challenged her complacency about seeking truth for the sake of her soul. Was Christianity true? Or was her mother's search for enlightenment the way? The pastor explained to this searching soul her need of forgiveness before a holy God, and how Jesus' sacrifice provided a way to freely receive this mercy.

Forgiveness sounded good to Beatrice's mind. It was free, and she couldn't think of anything she could offer God anyway. She welcomed the idea that there was a Creator in control – though everything at the moment felt so chaotic. The simplicity of God's love for her tugged at Bani's second youngest daughter and triumphed. She bowed her head and offered God her heart, which was all she had to give. Beatrice finally succumbed to the sleep she needed, content that whatever happened now would be in God's tender care.

Days later the unthinkable happened as the bombs dropped over Taunggyi. Ukanbu left the valley with his cart after the family watched in horror as their home town suffered enormous destruction. The fires were still burning as Emmerline's uncle made his way in disbelief through the carnage and casualties the Japanese had inflicted so quickly. The fact became obvious that in advancing this far, the Japanese were maintaining air superiority over the British; Ukanbu surmised that ground troops would soon be advancing to the top of the crag. Arriving at his mother's house, Ukanbu was enveloped by sheer relief as soon as Esther, and Bani's two children were in sight. Thankfully, not only his mother's house but also the house he'd built adjacent to it, were safe. God had answered the prayers of Sein's family for protection. Now they would need help processing the emotional aftermath of this sudden violence. They could no longer stay in Taunggyi. Taking Esther, and Bani's children, Ukanbu put his mother's house in order, considered and acquired whatever necessities they'd need during their displacement and piled everything into an ox cart. Before the week was over, the four manouevered back down the steep dirt road and into the valley to join the rest of the family at White Crow Lake.

This Karen family and many others were forced into an exodus to preserve their lives. The British and American missionaries working in Taunggyi sought safe haven in India. Friends of Sein's family, missionary Bill Hackett and his wife, Marion, found their escape route through China.[1] Dr L.T. Ah Pon, a national and co-worker of Dr Henderson's, chose not to leave Burma.

Half-Chinese and half-Burmese, Ah Pon's life before the war was a testimony to his Christian convictions, as he compassionately shared his medical skills and the gospel with the people in MuongNai and Taunggyi.[2] When the Japanese arrived, they took Ah Pon prisoner and pressured him to renounce his faith, as if the intruders could steal both his country *and* his faith. They didn't recognize Ah Pon's cover of armour – as a soldier under a different reign. He had no reason to abandon the Commander who had already won the real war.

Though kind and compassionate, the doctor's very presence threatened the inquisitors and they ordered his execution. Sein's family were told the Japanese killed Ah Pon, then ordered his grieving wife and three children to bury him.

Like Ah Pon, other nationals chose to stay in Burma, but not with the intention of fighting the Japanese. A number of Bamar volunteers joined the Burmese Independence Army (BIA), collaborating with the Japanese hoping to reclaim Burma from the British.[3] Burmese Indians, who were predominantly Hindu, had migrated to Taunggyi from British India during the British rule and many became proprietors. Like the BIA, the Indian National Army (INA) formed in 1942 as a movement to gain autonomy from the British.[4] Their alliance with Japan allowed the Indian business owners to live in relative safety as they managed their stores during the occupation.

Karen and other ethnic groups, however, aligned themselves with the British and Chinese (who joined the Allies in their own interests). Their forces were pushed back by the Japanese ground troops continually advancing north in spite of dense jungles, mountains and challenging rivers. Civilians, of course, ran anywhere to avoid the crossfire.

When Japanese soldiers entered Taunggyi, they deliberately created a front of terror to instil fear in the local people and subdue them. Christians were systematically identified as British allies, worthy of torture or death. The soldiers captured Sein's pastor and hung him – hands tied behind his back – from the roof of a building for three hours, eliciting excruciating pain. Eventually he was let loose and thrown into a single room with a number of other Christians. For three months, each day screamed uncertainty as the prisoners lived the monotony of their confinement. Their only relief was receiving two meals a day of rice and water. Out of earshot of his captors, Sein's pastor prayed for God's protection and liberation. On Christmas Day, a Japanese Christian soldier took pity on them and added curry to their rice. Soon after, the Japanese let down their guard and allowed the Christian prisoners to leave.

Sein's family found refuge close to White Crow Lake. Life outside of occupied Taunggyi offered optimism that displaced families out of the soldiers' sight were safe. Unbelievably, months passed without direct interference from anyone. Villagers could wash clothes or bathe in the cold lake. Food was still available. This blessing of living unmolested by invaders helped Beatrice convalesce from smallpox. Thankfully no one else in the family fell prey to the potentially fatal virus. Life seemed more manageable until a direct order came from the Japanese-controlled administration in Taunggyi, scrambling already shattered lives.

Following orders, soldiers arrived in Pan Gway and demanded that all children return with them to Taunggyi to attend school. This close family was again compelled to separate. To keep a low profile, their ageing grandmother Sein remained at the village with Ukanbu, Peh, Esther and Nan Yone. The aunts accompanied Bani's offspring and Peh's son, Andrew, as well as seven orphaned children who had come under the family's care before the war, to the plateau on the crag. The troops, anticipating the children's apprehension and inconsolable tears, requested they sing along the way. Onlookers would have viewed a curious sight – rifle-toting Japanese troops walking beside frightened children singing English and Burmese songs.

As they reached the plateau, the sight of Taunggyi's decimation was sobering. Even more appalling was the sight of the flag of the Rising Sun overhead and, more specifically, over their grandmother's house, commandeered and put to use as a war office. They could not return to the sheltered and secure compound that Sein and Maunggyi had established over four decades earlier. In fact, the Japanese compelled Sein's children and grandchildren to live in a designated area in the centre of Taunggyi, along with seventeen other Karen, Shan and Burmese families housed in similar circumstances.

Life in the centre of Taunggyi was relatively safe for the aunts and children as long as the enemy didn't suspect that they were spies, who attempted to remain faceless as they kept others well-informed of the up-to-date locations of troops or stories from the occupation – often relating the Japanese's campaign of terror in other villages.

One particularly gruesome story circulated about a group of twelve national pastors in the Hpapun village. They were ordered to dig a large pit for their own grave. As they were forced to lie down next to the hole, the Japanese sliced off their heads with long knives and threw their bodies into the mass grave. The traumatized villagers later recounted that they could still hear the pastors singing 'Nearer My God to Thee' long after they were buried. In the years to come, according to the local people, nothing ever grew over the place of their burial.

This terror crusade was not just sanctioned by the occupying Japanese. The BIA fighters attacked and killed the Karen in many of their rural villages and raped their defenceless women where few witnesses could substantiate the soldiers' brutality.[5]

In the centre of Taunggyi, there seemed to be some sort of attempt underway to restore a sense of normality. Due to their high levels of proficiencies, Gyi, Nge and Carmeline (now 20) found work in an office of the occupation forces. With the ABM schools closed by the Japanese, Emmerline, Beatrice, Jacqueline and the seven orphans attended a Japanese school where using

English was absolutely forbidden. Only the younger ones were allowed to attend school; the older children were forced to work on farms. Emmerline's older brothers, instead of working on these farms, worked in a butcher shop. The boys' collective salary was a stipend of rice, salt and oil every month. On a rare occasion they brought home a small portion of meat, providing a bit of much-needed protein in their diets.

Throughout Burma, Christians were prohibited from corporate worship.[6] If school buildings weren't destroyed, many were closed. Remarkably, the occupation army allowed one school still standing to be used as a church for worship services, frequented even by Christians of the Japanese military. For Bani's children, this corporate worship was like a refreshing drink in a parched land. But if the grandchildren of Sein thought they were on a hiatus from all the heartache, they were under the wrong impression.

Below the crag, the older adults in the family lived the daily struggles of an uprooted life. They were ever-mindful of how suddenly affairs can change. As if to emphasize this truth, Andrew's mother, Peh, having had stomach issues for some time, suddenly died. Much like her brother Bani, the diagnosis was indeterminate. With the war on, diagnostic equipment, medical personnel and medicines were for soldiers' care; civilians' health was not a priority.

The husband of Peh, Kyaw Wai, had passed away when Andrew was just 3 years old. Now, with the death of his surviving parent, Andrew was under the care of his aunts and Uncle Ukanbu. He became, to Bani's children, a bona fide brother – so much so that Emmerline would forget that he was a cousin. For Aunt Gyi and Aunt Nge, little change was required to care for this additional 12-year-old. Since returning to Taunggyi, they cared for Andrew and the other children, albeit on a smaller scale, given the grip of the Japanese. Overseeing growing boys in occupied Burma was becoming complicated as they confronted the new challenges.

One day, the Japanese ordered Hla Than and nine others to taxi troops to another village in ox carts. Thinking about 15-year-old Hla Than carrying out such an order, the older aunts and the children fought anxious hearts. This ruthless enemy had demanded drivers and carts before. Once the drivers reached their destination, the Japanese had kept the ox carts and massacred all of the men.

All of the Christians were sick with worry. They banded together to go on their knees because they knew Scripture taught that prayer was their greatest weapon. At 7 a.m. the next morning, as the group left the village, the Christians began to fast and pray. Much to their relief, by 7 p.m. that evening, Hla Than and his group returned with their ox carts.

If losing Peh wasn't enough of a burden, more difficulties occurred within the year. Esther awoke to an ache taking over her body. The subsequent telltale headache, chills and high fever told Esther she was in for a bout of malaria. Despite the treatment her family administered, Esther's chills increased and her ashen skin took on a yellow tinge. Her pale red urine darkened to black as if someone had infused charcoal in it – a sign of Blackwater fever. With Esther's countenance deathly, the family implored Aunt Gyi and Aunt Nge to hurry back to the village by White Crow Lake, bringing the children with them. Inside 11-year-old Emmerline's heart, a deep cavity of pain formed as she watched her dear Aunt Esther slip away. Though she and Esther had eluded the giant 'killer bees' of the Japanese attack, there was no hiding from the tiny malarial parasites that took her aunt's life.

Three days later, Aunt Gyi and Aunt Nge and the children had no choice but to return to the centre of Taunggyi. Whether above or below the great rock on which Taunggyi resided, this family of God clung to him in a very dark valley overshadowed by uncertainty. Nan Yone continued to live with Ukanbu and Sein, working diligently as days turned into months and months merged into the year 1944.

By the end of that year, the winds of war were shifting in favour of the Allies, whose armies had reorganized and were executing a successful counter-offensive to regain Burma. Word came from the spies that the Japanese were starting to evacuate. In order to avoid the inevitable bombing of Taunggyi, Sein's family loaded their ox cart and fled, this time to the small village of Loi-Kaung where they thought they would be safe.

7

At War's End Emmerline Becomes a Woman

Let us hold unswervingly to the hope we profess, for he who promised is faithful.

Hebrews 10:23

No longer a child but emerging into her teen years, Emmerline observed Loi-Kaung from her vantage point outside the village. She was glad to be reunited with family and away from Taunggyi as Allied planes targeted the city. On the upside, the village had a church where the Christians could worship; on the downside, Loi-Kaung stood next to a Japanese command post.

Emmerline and three other girls were assigned to watch the family's cows – precious commodities during a time of peace, let alone in time of war. The cows were especially important to her ageing grandmother Sein, for the old woman's only mode of movement was the ox cart as her family navigated dirt roads ravaged by holes, ruts and the effects of battle.

Emmerline watched absent-mindedly on the hill. A deep grunt erupted from one of the Brahman cows while another moved its head up and down, tearing grass from the chestnut-coloured dirt – both animals oblivious to the tug-of-war pulling Burma apart. While she watched their antics,

Emmerline heard the familiar and unsettling low pitch of planes above.

The girls squinted as they looked for the recognizable red emblem on the approaching four planes. Astonished, they saw a white star on royal blue emblazoned on the silver metal shining back at them. The planes of the United States Army Air Force opened their bellies and were dropping bombs over Loi-Kaung! All three girls sprinted towards the canopy of the largest tree offering cover. Helplessly they watched the incoming attack.

Uncle Ukanbu and Emmerline's youngest sister, Jacqueline, were on their way back from another village when the commotion overhead startled them. Ukanbu glanced anxiously at 5-year-old Jacqueline. She claimed a special place in his heart as his brother Bani's youngest child. In his sixties, Ukanbu had become like a grandfather to Jacqueline and often teased her when he could elicit a reaction. One time, having discovered her love for noodles, Ukanbu decided to play the antagonist. He heaped the coveted rice pasta on everyone's plate but hers. She got only 3. Her loud protests sent family members into gales of laughter. With bombs falling on Loi-Kaung, he wasn't teasing as he yelled at Jacqueline to jump with him over an embankment and into the dry streambed for protection. Then he threw his body over Jacqueline, keeping her safe from the explosions and shrapnel ripping through the air.

As the attack continued, one bomb dropped in line with the church building. Wide-eyed, Emmerline watched as it burst in mid-air over the church – a miracle, she surmised, because it left the building undisturbed. Later that day, the Japanese and Burmese investigated damages to the village. They found eleven craters where bombs had exploded and were astonished to learn there was not a single loss of life. The entire community, which was largely Christian, met later at the unscathed church building to thank and praise God for their safety. Among the worshippers was Sein, relieved for her family's safekeeping in the attack but instinctively aware of its foreboding message. Hitching the cows to the ox cart one more time, her family left in search of a different sanctuary that would be unnoticed by the advancing British and retreating Japanese.

Civilians were never certain if one settlement was safer than another, but the family chose Thada Mei Laung (Burnt Bridge) as their next refuge. Uprooting always necessitated the search for temporary shelter, a place to worship and a reasonable amount of food to eat. If refugees couldn't buy or barter food from the villagers, they foraged in the Burma forests or jungles – the dry or rainy season dictating what was available. At times, they were fortunate, finding mangos, papaya, durian, jackfruit, bananas, edible leaves, duck eggs, pheasant or an occasional jungle fowl. The longer the war, the scarcer the food became, so it was good news when the spies announced the British and their allies were finally pushing the Japanese back.

After five months, Sein's family heard that Taunggyi was back in British hands. Soon they were again listening to the bullock cart's creaking as its driver manoeuvred through the diverse terrain. This time their departure was not an evacuation from terror. With high hopes of a truce between the warring factions, the Sein family left with a happier countenance. When they saw an occasional fleet of American flyers overhead, family members enthusiastically waved their white handkerchiefs. No one wanted to be mistaken for the Japanese.

As Sein's family and others drew closer to Taunggyi, American GIs met them on the road and generously handed out chocolate as a demonstrative token of friendship. The chocolate, melting in the children's mouths, put them in a celebratory mood. But the worn-out travellers quickly abandoned their jovial mood as they crested the crag and took in the sight of war-riddled Taunggyi. The scarred landscape screamed the in- justice of forces from two foreign countries fighting it out on Burma's soil.

The family's return to their compound brought more bad news. The Japanese had burned Sein's home to the ground be- fore they retreated, destroying whatever plans or maps might have been left behind. Thankfully, Ukanbu's house still stood and would serve as their new home and give them an opportu- nity to reorganize their lives. For a few weeks, war planes flew overhead, monitoring any unusual activity in Taunggyi. Then a day came when the planes left and never returned. In the after- math, churches, schools, government buildings, Shan palaces and pagodas were damaged or completely lost. The war's survi- vors – whether Buddhist or Christian, Shan or Karen – needed to pull together at this time and rebuild their lives.

The wages of war begot more needy children who began to arrive at Sein's doorstep to join the other seven previously in her care. No child was turned away even though the war propagated a shortage of many basic provisions. The destroyed infrastructure crippled the country's roads, and transporting food became a logistical challenge. Sesame oil was more plen- tiful in the central part of Burma while rice was more available in the delta. Clothes were difficult to find, since Burma pro- duced very little cotton. This Karen family took one step, one day at a time, reminding God that he was their source to meet these needs.

After the war's end schools were re-established, which sent the children within the care of Sein's family back to their ed- ucation and the spinster aunts back to teaching. Learning brought a sense of order for Emmerline, who was enrolled in

the Standard 8 at the government school. The next two years
flew by in the busyness of schoolwork and responsibilities of
a large household. Emmerline and the other girls learned to
sew handkerchiefs, tablecloths and napkins, intricately stitching in forget-me-nots, daisies and roses. These were practical
skills useful in earning money. By the time she reached 15,
Emmerline balanced attending Standard 10 with helping to
teach the kindergarteners at an ABM school. The next year she
began teaching kindergarten at the government school.

Like a butterfly emerging from its cocoon, Emmerline left
her childhood as she was transformed from student to instruc-
tor. Now the children respectfully used the name '*Theramu*'
(teacher). Growing up had brought a new liberty in thinking
about what she believed and wanted. The young adult didn't
realize this fresh independence would be tested so soon. Without warning, the changing woman encountered a crossroad in
her life, and his name was Jan Bahadur.

Emmerline's acquaintance with Jan Bahadur came from
their government school days together. She hadn't thought
much about him until now. Jan lived with his widowed
mother. Though about the same age, he attended Standard 10
in the school where Emmerline taught. Young people tend to
gravitate towards each other, and they were no different, soon
finding themselves in amicable conversations. He was handsome, with dark eyes and a tall frame, just as she was beautiful,
talented and quite sociable. In an ambience of renewed hope
shaping Taunggyi, an undeniable fondness began to form between them.

The two friends began meeting for lunch on school days.
This tall and good-looking young man was so kind and intel-
ligent that Emmerline wanted to see him more often than on
her work days. To her it was reasonable to think of possibly

becoming his wife. After all, her older sister, Suzaline, had an ample number of suitors competing for her affection. She wondered, musing on her mother's marriage at the age of 16, if the time had come for her to get married. But there was one unmistakable problem, a huge hurdle really – Jan Bahadur was a Hindu.

The raging battling in her Christian heart was as real as Burma's past conflicts. Emmerline loved her elders and she knew they would not approve of someone – Nan Yone, for example – of a different faith. At the age of 8, Emmerline had been born again;[1] she had accepted the free gift of forgiveness and restoration that Christ provides. Now her heart clung to God even more than she clung to her family. Reading the Bible was an illumination into God's heart and what he thought about his children living 'yoked together with unbelievers'[2] – like a Brahman cow and water buffalo hitched to the same ox cart. But she also loved Jan Bahadur. Emmerline knew that if they were to marry, their compatibility would end with their friendship; it would not grow into a spiritual union.

Her deep faith professed a God of love who created her and everything good, not a universal god who appeared in many idolatrous forms. It was God, not karma, who had the last say in her life. One day she would stand before him and give account[3] for whatever choices she made on earth. There was no point discussing this with her family. Praying for courage, this determined young lady knew what she had to do and there was no turning back.

The next time they met, Emmerline told Jan Bahadur that she was breaking off their relationship. Devastated, he continued to come to her for a couple of months, pleading with her to reconsider. But her answer was always the same. Eventually he stopped coming.

The break-up brought so much grief that Emmerline spent hours crying. Then to comfort herself she would eat, cry and eat again until her tears returned. This never helped the grief to go away, so one day she decided that God was well aware of her situation and he must have a plan that would bring her more joy than being married to her friend. Surely, the joy of this future life was just around the corner.

But a different plot was developing. In the aftermath of the war, Burma's political scene changed fast. On 4 January 1948, British control over Burma ended. The Burmans, the Buddhist majority who had been pushing against colonization by Britain for years, were elated. It would be disastrous, however, for the Karens who had sided with the British, not only in the First World War, but in the previous Anglo-Burmese wars that gave Britain control of the country. The Karen had looked to the British as a means of gaining their own autonomy. In 1947 the British approved formation of the Karen National Union (KNU), authorizing as well the flag and national anthem of the Karen. The KNU proceeded to form a military, the Karen National Liberation Army. The KNU-KNLA then began to push for its own Karen State.[4]

Intertwined in the breach of these two ethnicities was the division between Buddhism and Christianity, though not all Burmans were Buddhists, nor were all Karen Christian. Neither religion promoted violence. The religious differences between the two ethnic groups only added to the power struggle and accentuated an ever-growing divide between dreams in what people wanted for their beloved Burma. Rather than differences being resolved through meetings and concessions, violence escalated, with a developing distrust between the two sides. One year after British rule ended, the Burmese government and the Karen were in a civil war.

8

The Family Flees Further Violence

Have I not commanded you? Be strong and courageous.
Do not be afraid; do not be discouraged, for the LORD
your God will be with you wherever you go.

Joshua 1:9

The year 1949 in Burma began what some sources consider the world's longest running civil war in modern history.[1] Two years earlier, in 1947, the Anti-Fascist People's Freedom League (AFPFL) – a political union of different parties originally formed to combat the Japanese – had won the country's national elections. In seeking a unified Burma, the AFPFL reorganized and strengthened the armed forces, the Tatmadaw, to suppress any opposition. The Karen did not align with this newly established government, believing they would not be allowed their own autonomous Karen State.[2] (This, even though a newer version of the country's constitution indeed did recognize Karen State.) A growing rift and continual tensions between Burmans and the Karen created outbreaks of fighting in communities inhabited by both ethnic groups. Escalation of such skirmishes and the formal announcement of the civil war unnerved Sein's family, punctuating the urgency for their family to run . . . again.

This time the Karen family chose to find refuge in Papun (Hpapun). They assumed that the Tatmadaw would not venture there, for it was deep within insurgent territory. Arrangements were made for the children under their care to return to available relatives. Seven remaining orphaned children were left with people of the Pa-O tribe – three siblings who had been gardeners for Sein's family.

Before their departure, the family gathered items difficult to buy, such as towels, as a means for bartering. For sustenance on the journey, they stuffed cooked dried rice and bits of other food into small bags placed in their pockets. Their large trunk bulged with rice, blankets, pillows and other necessary items for the 225-mile journey and the prospective stay in Papun. Suzaline, now the wife of Kyaw Nyunt, and her older brothers had previously moved to Rangoon. They didn't join the rest of the family when they left the great crag and went down through the valley to find safety in the jungle.

Packed tightly into a car, the evacuees were driven to Loikaw, and then on to Mawchi in a relatively uneventful trip. Papun, on the other hand, lay on the west side of the Salween River. The family's destination required that they employ four Shan men who could navigate a wide boat capable of handling the notorious and threatening Salween.

Once they found the riverbank, this family of nine, the four Shan and their plethora of possessions took off in a wide wooden boat. At first the water seemed to cooperate as the four Shan simultaneously worked their oars. But the current soon became swift and hazardous, rendering the oars useless. Needing concentration and focus, one of the Shan men ordered those on board to stay quiet as they approached perilous rapids and an exceedingly violent vortex through a passageway of grand boulders and rocks. Family members lifted silent prayers, pleading for safety as they were jerked, tossed and see-sawed through the convulsive waters.

The drenched passengers were shaking but intact as the boat pushed on to more tranquil water. Sein and her family were thankful when they came to an area of the riverbank where they could dry off, leave the boat and spend the night. The last leg of the journey was too far for Sein to walk or for the others to carry their well-filled, heavy trunk. Heaving the family matriarch and the possessions onto the barrel-shaped backs of elephants became the only available solution. The elderly grandmother swayed from side to side, hanging on, while the rest of her family walked.

Reaching Papun, the delighted itinerant family discovered two established churches. From Taunggyi they had brought with them their Bibles and hymnbooks, and were ready to worship and socialize with the other believers. Though their many flights from danger to haven meant hardship, the sweet fellowship with other Christians took the bitterness from their wandering. The Karen needed schoolteachers, so they especially welcomed the aunts and eldest sister to their village.

One Karen man gave the new family a large house. It could serve not only for living quarters but also for a private school. Before they had even settled in, their shovels were out, pitching dirt into the air as they carved out a trench for a new bomb shelter. Each time the clan of Sein entered a village, their number one task before any other business was digging the protective air-raid refuge. Before long, the aunts and sisters were teaching 100 students in the manner they had learned from the ABM and government schools – where teaching English or the Bible carried no reprisals. Fees paid to the school became, for the family, a blessing to supplement their needs.

What wasn't grown by the villagers – such as sweet and sour pineapples and bananas in various shades of red, green and yellow – could be found in the wild. Nan Yone and her daughters found the jungle a valuable hunting venue. . . if they were careful. The tropical jungles of Burma stood in contrast to the forested crag that the family had left behind. Emmerline volunteered to explore the jungle with her basket and knife, scouting for tropical trees hanging with fruit or edible leaves for added nutrition in their diet. If she wasn't foraging for fruit, she took a single-barrelled shotgun to hunt an unsuspecting fowl. One night, Ukanbu caught the glowing eyes of a tiger and brought it down with his double-barrelled shotgun. There wasn't any meat they turned away – including that of an occasional dog or cat.

The jungle, though, had a way of fighting back. Avoiding bamboo groves housing black scorpions and staying alert for cobras and pythons quietly slithering beneath the tangled overgrowth was common sense. Some days were unsettling for Emmerline when she was alone, cutting twigs and branches for firewood. She felt more secure with her younger sisters, Beatrice and Jacqueline, as companions under the flourishing canopy.

Even something as innocuous as cutting down fruit from a tree potentially exposed them to danger. One day, the three young women carefully climbed a tree, hoping for a good harvest. Concentrating intently on the mission at hand, they did not notice the movement under their roost. Bagging the coveted fruit, they hopped down and were startled to discover a bear nearby, rummaging for his own reward. The three promptly ran the race of their lives and somehow managed to escape him.

Avoiding such dangers wasn't always possible. On a previous occasion, a youth had followed Emmerline out of the village, curious about her endeavours. After walking a distance, she found a tree loaded with yellow fruit. To reach this bounty, the fruit-picker manoeuvred the branches until she found a safe position to cut her prize. While she was safely up in the tree, a wild boar came through and viciously attacked the defenceless boy below. The predator was swift, and even though the boy ran to the tree, he was fatally gored in the back and stomach. Horrified Emmerline could do nothing to help him.

The family's greatest fear, however, wasn't the indigenous animal life of the jungle's fauna and flora. The animals, at least, were not intentionally stalking humans, as were the government forces intent on driving out opposition in Burma. The Karen people took great measures to avoid the soldiers, who might appear unannounced at any moment.

Each night a rhythmic thumping reverberated throughout the area because the villagers prudently waited until dark to pound rice in the mortars with their pestles. Military attacks would most likely not come under the light of the moon. During the day, they kept a heightened awareness for any sound that indicated incoming planes. Deep in Karen territory, as months were turning into years, Sein's family could never know when sporadic fighting between the Tatmadaw and the opposition would arrive at their doorstep.

During her time in Papun, Emmerline began work as a medical assistant to Dr J. Po. Though she had no previous medical knowledge, the doctor needed help. Thankful for the work, Emmerline found that it enabled her to learn about the uses and dosages of medicines. She travelled to other villages, exchanging medicines and medical assistance for rice and vegetables. One needed staple difficult to forage for in the jungle, shoot with a rifle or grow in the garden, was soap. It had to come through the backroads of neighbouring Thailand.

In the mostly Christian Karen village of Papun, Nan Yone – Shan and Buddhist – was always busily serving others. She would wake up very early to take care of anything that her no-nagenarian mother-in-law, Sein, couldn't do for herself. Or she would help her brother-in-law, Ukanbu, who was advancing into his senior years. When she wasn't cooking, cleaning, or gathering food, the humble daughter-in-law spent time reading her Shan Bible.

Like the tug-of-war for power in Burma, Nan Yone's heart had been torn for many years between the truths of the Bible and the precepts of Buddhism. It seemed that Buddhists, like Hindus, were striving ultimately to relieve their *own* suffering. Whether adhering to righteous acts in fear of karma or believing separating themselves from desires and attachments could make their suffering cease to exist, the people struggled to be free. Jesus, on the other hand, selflessly and purposely *chose* suffering on Nan Yone's behalf. He didn't run away from it.

It would have made more sense if God had completely destroyed humanity when they chose their own way, rather than sending his Son to give his life for a race of rebels. All of Burma was a living witness to the devastating violence between men who demanded their own way. But 'God so loved the world', she read in her Bible, 'that he gave his one and only Son'[3] . . . At the age of 60, and at a critical juncture in her life, Nan Yone chose Christianity over her long-held Buddhism. She had wearied of the anxiety that controlled her view of life and had tired of the interminable demand of karma. Most importantly, she rejected the lie that the antidote to evil was her own goodness.

When Nan Yone had first joined her husband's family, she felt alienated from her sisters-in-law who questioned her religion, her minimal education, her Shan language and ethnicity. But like the Samaritan woman in the Bible's New Testament who felt estranged from God's people,[4] this Buddhist mother discovered Jesus' unconditional love waiting for her. The revelation of this wonder captured her heart.

Nan Yone's and Bani's youngest daughter, the one he never had a chance to know, also made a decision to follow Jesus. Jacqueline and her now Christian mother were baptized in a nearby stream – a statement to the world of their commitment. The village believers were rejoicing in this good news when another announcement came their way.

During the family's six years in Papun, Sein's granddaughters had grown from their teen years into womanhood. All had reached marriageable age – a fact not ignored by fellow churchgoer, Saw Dickson. Both a Karen and a Christian, he was an ideal bachelor for any of the girls in this small community. His choice of a bride turned out to be sweet-natured Beatrice, who was impressed with this single man seven years her junior.

Nan Yone was very agreeable to Saw Dickson's proposal of marriage, even though it meant the new couple would leave the Karen village. This marriage not only changed her daughter's life, but her life as well. She had drafted an addendum to the marriage arrangement, requesting that her new son-in-law and his bride take her to live with them in Rangoon. It was a commitment they were more than happy to make.

Nan Yone had been submissive to her husband's mother, her brother-in-law and her sisters-in-law for over thirty-three years. Now that her youngest was 18, she considered her duty to her husband, Bani, fulfilled. When it was time for the newlyweds to start their new life in southern Burma, their mother-in-law accompanied them with a lighter heart and a lighter step – that of one who had just been given her autonomy.

In contrast, gaining independence was not within easy reach of the Karen who were still fighting the government forces, the Tatmadaw. A day of great consternation came when the residents of Papun heard a loud shrill noise overhead, announcing enemy planes. Emmerline, the strongest of all the grandchildren, had been designated as the one to carry Sein into the trenches should it become necessary.

Indeed, now it was necessary, but her grandmother was not willing to go. At 98, she was frail, tired and not clear-minded. She had developed, like so many others, a habit of chewing the betel nut – which was very addictive. Instead of allowing her granddaughter to carry her to safety, the elderly woman insisted on retrieving her betel nut. Emmerline, the stronger of the two, won the argument and carried her to the trench before the explosions began.

The frightened family left before the Tatmadaw completely overran Papun. Though by now it was safe to return to Taunggyi, they chose to scout out another small jungle village. It would be risky to transport Sein, now sickly and frail, by boat back to Mawchi in order to return to their home above the crag. They loaded their belongings and again climbed on the backs of elephants, which sauntered slowly through the jungle as the family looked for the best place to establish themselves.

Emmerline refused to ride an elephant, rationalizing she was too strong and healthy to need one – though at times the walking put her in a stream as high as her neck. The water at least offered a reprieve from the intense heat of the jungle now that it was the dry season. The family first settled in Saw Pweh Der and stayed there for a year before moving on to Hsa Pu Pey. After two months, news came that the Tatmadaw had entered the area, so they left for Thay Doe Kwee. Bittersweet news awaited them just as the end of their wanderings was in sight.

Sein, the matriarch of this extraordinary family, the lady with a huge heart and compassion for the children of Burma, died at the age of 100 in 1957. Her life was like a beacon, brightening a road that her children could choose to follow. But would they follow? That would be the question Emmerline and her family would ask themselves as they travelled back north to Taunggyi.

9

The Daw Gyi Daw Nge Orphanage and Old People's Home

For the LORD God is a sun and shield; the LORD bestows favour and honour; no good thing does he withhold from those whose way of life is blameless.

Psalm 84:11

Though the precarious boat trip down the Salween River previously had taken one day, the trip going north took three. Just as the oars were useless when the Shan oarsmen approached the swift waters downstream, the same wooden paddles were impractical as they fought the powerful current upstream. The men guided the boat near the shallow riverbank so that, if they needed to, they could hop out and push while trudging through the silt. The slowness of the task accentuated Emmerline's anxiousness to get back to Taunggyi.

When the newly bereaved family of Sein returned to their home on the crag, friends and neighbours greeted them with dishes, blankets, food and other practical necessities. This unexpected kindness was a blessing, as they had given away most of their possessions during their nomadic journey through the villages. Once they were settled, a decision needed to be made concerning the children of Burma – the legacy left by their recently deceased matriarch.

The answer wasn't long in coming. A view through their window revealed eighteen underprivileged children playing and giggling inside Ukanbu's home, framing the family's decision to continue the tradition set before them. The constant challenge was how to provide for their ever-growing needs. The answer highlighted their entrepreneurial spirit.

The schoolteachers – Gyi, Nge and Emmerline's oldest sister, Carmeline – made the decision to build their own school. The ambitious women started the process of building with whatever natural resources were available to them around Taunggyi. Wood was plentiful and it was a medium they could handle. What these female constructors couldn't do for themselves, they hired people to do. Once their money ran out, they secured a loan from the government (rather than risk the high interest rate of unethical moneylenders) for the sake of finishing the schoolhouse. Crediting and thanking God for his provision, they paid off the loan within a couple of years.

When the private school opened in 1958, it was designed for ages 5 to 14. The younger grades filled up the classes first, but as the years went on and children graduated from one class to the next, the school was bursting with 200 children. Emmerline resumed teaching kindergarten while her aunts, sisters and hired teachers taught other grades. English would be a priority for the children to learn.

During the time of British colonial rule, if a student could speak English, they had a higher chance of receiving a government or professional job. After the war, they recognized that more books were written in English than Burmese and if they wanted their students to expand their horizons, understanding English was paramount. English, arithmetic, reading and writing were designed to be a part of the curriculum.

Though these industrious women busied themselves with teaching the students at school and tending to all the children at their home, five more children arrived after completion of the school building. The older aunts and sisters taught Christian principles through Bible stories and their favourite hymns or choruses. Teaching prayer was tantamount, as the oversight of such a large number of children certainly required an Overseer much greater than they.

Generally, their charges were rarely ill because exposure to germs in close quarters built up their immune systems. Slight bruises, mild cuts and bumps or an occasional broken bone accompanied the territory of children navigating their rough-and-tumble world. It was surprising then, when an orphanage boy's complaint of stomach pain persisted.

Duly distressed, little Abraham's pale face winced as he bent over while sitting in class. On the onset of his illness, he appeared to have flu-like symptoms – vomiting and diarrhoea. But as the day progressed, so did the unrelenting pain and fever. More worrisome, his belly continued to swell and he grew increasingly weaker. Finally awake to the fact that something was not right, Emmerline and her sisters carried the sick child to the hospital, seeking professional help. After some poking, prodding and testing, the attending physician diagnosed a twisted colon. The doctor went out of the room to make arrangements for the emergency surgery. But before the surgeon's knife was on the table, little Abraham's life slipped away. Everything shared in this orphanage now included this common bereavement. Yet this was only a foreshadowing of more loss to come. The turmoil defining Burma was hardly over.

U Nu became Premier of Burma as the leader of the AFPFL. General U Ne Win was appointed Chief of Staff of the Armed Forces, which gave him complete control of the Tatmadaw. The AFPFL became increasingly politically divided and the split resulted in a weak government.[1] Taking advantage of this weakness, General Ne Win led a coup d'état on 2 March 1962, replacing the elected government with complete military control.

The new military regime swiftly slammed the door to other political influences and interference from outside Burma. In a quest to bring the country into unity, independence for any one ethnic group was denied.[2] This dictatorial style government instigated socialism, which seemed to hold to the ideals of Buddhism.[3] Without understanding the military's future intentions, and wanting the country to be unified after the upheaval of the previous years, many Burmese were indifferent to the takeover.[4] The years under General Ne Win took Burma from being one of the richest Asian countries to the United Nations adding it to the 'Least Developed Countries' list.[5] Countless institutions were eliminated or nationalized, forcing private schools to close down, except for a few Buddhist monastic schools in rural areas.[6] All foreigners were forced out of the country, so missionaries had to return home or move to another field in a different country. Schools were only allowed to teach in Burmese, not English.

By 1966, Emmerline's family was forced to close their school. The aunts chose to tutor privately in their home. The three sisters had no choice: if they were going to teach, they would do so in the government school under Ne Win's control.

Ukanbu – now well into his eighties – had lived long enough to see Bani's children become responsible adults. He could see that Carmeline, Emmerline and Jacqueline carried in their hearts the family's legacy to protect the children of Burma. Satisfied that his job was finished, the benevolent and good-natured uncle laid his head down and quietly died as another wave of violence threatened to engulf Burma.

Ne Win, in his quest for unifying the government, began a campaign with a 'Four Cuts' strategy to put down rebel insurgencies. The goal was to cut off food, finance, intelligence and recruits to the ethnic opposition armies.[7] This resulted in violent government attacks on the Karen and other ethnic minority groups. This increase in brutality left many civilians dead or impoverished when their villages and farms were burned to the ground. The most vulnerable and innocent – the children – suffered in the aftermath, often losing parents to death.

These indigent and orphaned children started arriving at Emmerline's family home. In 1970, the increasing numbers brought about the construction of an official orphanage building adjacent to the house Ukanbu had built. It was an effort in sheer determination and love. The family often recalled to mind the Bible verse from Philippians 4:13: 'I can do all this through him [Christ] who gives me strength.'

The orphanage building was completed in a year. Though it had been previously known as the 'Lakeville Home' during Sein's era, the name changed to the 'Daw Gyi Daw Nge Orphanage and Old People's Home'. When the new facility opened its doors, sixty children called it home. The family's finances and faith would be like a new bowstring pulled tight to hit its target.

Emmerline, her aunts and her sisters worked a variety of jobs to sustain the orphanage. The aunts and sisters tutored privately, teaching English or music lessons. On a Singer treadle sewing machine, the women worked long hours sewing clothes or meticulously stitching with needle and thread to create colourful floral designs on crisp white linens. Friends or former orphanage children stopped by and purchased the pleasing handicrafts or brought rice, eggs or money to help out. God faithfully and generously provided – often at the last minute. The never-ending work was exhausting. Emmerline developed a habit of being able to sleep almost anywhere at any time, whether she was sitting up or in the middle of a conversation. If another child came to their door, the family would adjust and add one more.

Even before the orphanage building was completed, a chubby and happy little 2-year-old appeared at their doorstep in the arms of a village chief. His parents had passed away and an aunt was not able to care for him. He was such a chubby little butterball that Emmerline's family decided to name him 'Ball'. Ball quickly became a favourite among the caregivers. By the time he was 4, he liked to accompany Emmerline to church. Then, without any warning, Ball started complaining of pain in his head. This soon developed into a pattern of headaches, which caused alarm. Emmerline took Ball to a medical clinic but the physician couldn't diagnose his illness; they had no other choice but to bring him home.

One night, Ball asked Emmerline to hold him, as his head was especially hurting and he was feeling very weak. Scooping him up in her lap, she held him close as if his life depended on it. But she couldn't stop the inevitable; little Ball died in her arms. After his death, the doctors were able to ascertain that a brain tumour had taken his young life. Though there were many other children in their care, losing little Ball was heartbreaking. Still, there was little time to mourn and reminisce because so many needed help.

The women not only cared for children but also for the old people who needed assistance. Usually the elderly had no family to care for them – and if their health allowed it, they remained in their own home while the aunts or the sisters brought them food and medicine and helped with other practical needs.

The thriving orphanage became well-known in Taunggyi and the surrounding area. Gyi and Nge, though quite elderly at this time, continued to tutor.

A student started coming consistently to get help in her school work, accompanied by her 2-year-old nephew. Jacqueline thought this little boy was unusually beautiful, with his very round face. The toddler became attached to her and all the 'mothers' in the orphanage as he trailed after them rather than preferring his own aunt. It soon became apparent that the little boy didn't want to leave, and Emmerline's family didn't want to let him go. The child's family – who were poor and struggling to care for their other children – agreed to give their son up to Jacqueline and her family. Rather than just taking him in like the other children, the aunts and sisters legally adopted him. Joining this enthusiastic and efficacious family, the new adoptee didn't realize at the time exactly how large this household had become and what significance this would play in his future.

10

Wingate, the Only Adopted Child

So do not worry, saying, 'What shall we eat?' or 'What shall we drink?' or 'What shall we wear?' For the pagans run after all these things, and your heavenly Father knows that you need them. But seek first his kingdom and his righteousness, and all these things will be given to you as well.

Matthew 6:31–33

This new dependant, and youngest member of Emmerline's family, was named Wingate, a name perhaps inspired by a British Army brigadier, Orde Charles Wingate, who had fought the Japanese in Burma during the Second World War more than two decades earlier. He was renowned for promoting a tough mental attitude. Mental toughness would be needed for this child adopted into the family. He would be competing with the other children in the crowded orphanage.

Wingate didn't find it unusual having so many siblings that they could field six soccer teams. And although he adjusted to having Gyi, Nge, Carmeline, Emmerline and Jacqueline as five nurturing mothers, he did struggle with five sets of expectations of him – expectations that exceeded the ones that every other orphanage child needed to meet.

Like something to be inherited, correct manners and etiquette that the caregivers had learned from Sein were in turn handed to Wingate. While the other orphanage children were taught to eat with a spoon and not chopsticks, their only legally adopted son was taught to eat with a knife, fork and spoon.

On rare occasions, they indulged Wingate by taking him to a movie theatre. The screen overhead starred a tough and rugged John Wayne, later impersonated by the little daydreamer. Wide-eyed, he would watch the tall cowboy hold a cup of coffee in one hand, his piece of fried chicken in the other, defying rules of proper etiquette. After he had seen that, the imitator insisted that he, too, would hold his tea in one hand and his food in the other. Like other parents, the doting women bought fun presents – a cowboy hat, a holster set and cowboy boots – for this special child. He possessed everything he could possibly need to become an American hero.

The children's education was handled in rooms of the government's institutions since all private, and the ABM's schools, had been closed. General Ne Win had established himself as Burma's president, and his takeover caused the country's educational standards to suffer. To supplement the children's learning, Carmeline taught Wingate and a few other willing orphanage children to play piano or sing.

Ma Than Htway, though three years his senior, became a close confidante of Wingate. Like others of his adoptive Karen family, he was musically gifted. Wingate played the piano and Ma Than Htway accompanied him with her appealing and clear voice. The fact that he was set apart from the rest of the children didn't seem to bother him, and he retained a humble attitude despite his unusual circumstances.

Like all the children, Wingate was taught the precepts of Christianity. All humans sin and fall short of God's glory,[1]

resulting in death and separation from God. His only Son,
Jesus, came to earth, taking on the form of a man to change
the outcome of people's eternal destiny. This humble Messiah
took upon Himself the penalty required for sin. He died on
a cross offering salvation to those who by faith would accept
the gift of eternal life. At the age of 8, Wingate welcomed this
free gift of salvation through a simple prayer of repentance and
was baptized. He then wanted to use his musical abilities for
God's glory. At a Sunday morning church service, Carmeline
accompanied him on the piano. As his family beamed in sheer
admiration, he sang his first solo in church, 'Open the Gates
of Jerusalem'.[2]

In the years to come, the memories imprinted in Wingate's
heart were of a loving but very large family. Topping his treas-
ured times of the year was Christmas, when family members
sat around the Christmas tree opening whatever gifts they had
been able to afford. The Christmas carols they sang in buoy-
ant and immaculate harmonies brought tears to his eyes. These
sweet moments, like all good memories, balanced harder years
that would soon come.

Nature's fraternal twins, the mountaintops and valleys, seem
to jostle for one's dominant view of life's landscape. After just a
few years of reprieve, another valley was coming into view. In
1979 in Rangoon, Nan Yone died at the home of her daughter Beatrice, bringing sorrow to her family as only a mother's
death can. Within a year after that, Suzaline suddenly passed
away. She left behind a husband and their three offspring. Gyi
and Nge also died, leaving responsibility for the underprivileged children in the hands of the three unmarried sisters –
Carmeline, Emmerline and Jacqueline.

Over the next few years, the economy as well as the rights
of ethnic minorities were under duress in an increasingly

impoverished country. Totalitarian in its governance, the Burma Socialist Programme Party (BSPP) demanded isolation from the rest of the world. This worsened Burma's economic status, pushing the country further into debt and forcing many into poverty.

Underlying animosities among Burma's people were a powder keg ready to explode with the slightest spark. In an attempt to wipe out the financial backing of his enemy insurgencies, President Ne Win made the 50- and 100-kyat notes of Burma's currency illegal and worthless, thus wiping out the savings of many. Superstitious, in 1987 he codified the advice of an astrologer, outlawing banknotes of 25, 35 and 75 kyat. Once illegal, notes could not be exchanged for legal currency. Ne Win allowed circulation of only 45 and 90-kyat notes, simply because they were divisible by nine.[3]

The Burmese lost their entire savings, including many pro-democratic university students whose anger was directed at Ne Win's socialistic government and the BSPP.

Student protests – sporadic on various Burma campuses since the mid-sixties – stepped up in intensity in 1987–88. Pressure from the protests prompted Ne Win to resign as BSPP chair, taking away his overt power as leader of the military dictatorship, which offered no improvements towards democracy or multiparty elections.

On 8 August 1988, student protests in Rangoon spread throughout the country. The military's response resulted in the deaths of thousands, although the government denies the high mortality numbers. Additionally, many were imprisoned or fled to Burma's border with India or Thailand. The protests, known as the 8888 Uprising, lasted until 18 September, when another military-led power, the State Law and Order Restoration Council (SLORC), took power in a violent coup.[4] Burma was ultimately plunged into a greater financial crisis. The SLORC, an unelected military junta, changed Burma's name to Myanmar and Rangoon's name to Yangon in 1989.[5]

The effects of these years were monumental on the three women left to tend the children. Lawlessness in Taunggyi forced people to protect their possessions from robbers and looters. With schools and businesses closed, jobs became difficult to find. The orphanage doubled as a school as Emmerline and her sisters became its instructors again. Even more frightening, the military was quick to point their guns at anyone deemed threatening.

Food rationing in Taunggyi began at the same time as the orphanage population swelled to 140 children. In an act to keep the children, Emmerline and her sisters started selling their valuables. Away went their jewellery and watches, the hand and treadle Singer sewing machines that had straight-stitched their clothes and provided income, and any number of other inherited possessions of worth. With their cupboards almost bare, they served watered-down rice. But no child was turned away.

On a brisk winter morning, Emmerline heard a little whimper, much like that of a bird in distress. Mystified, she finally woke up to the fact that the pitiful sound was coming from the family's front gate. Hurrying down to the street, she discovered a lovely and fair 2-month-old baby girl covered in a beautiful cloth. She was propped up in a rattan basket between a soft pillow, bottle of milk and baby powder. It was apparent that whoever had left her would not return.

The name Snow was given to this new gift entrusted to the orphanage. As if to defy the chaos in the world she was born into, the abandoned orphan grew up to graduate from high school with English and maths honours. She then attended nursing school and married a doctor. Her success is a testimony of God's care by this indomitable family in Burma.

The disturbing times around them never restrained the sisters' faith; there were too many in need to nurse despair. With the resources God provided, the three entrepreneurs opened 'Blue Heaven', a tea shop on their property. Wingate – now older – and another orphanage young man managed the small eatery, serving fried bread, coffee and tea cultivated in the Shan hills. This gathering place to converse with friends attracted local residents and students. However, tea shops also inadvertently provided a hot spot for undercover spies to listen in on any unauthorized and disgruntled conversations against the government. Inevitably, the police arrested at their small café two students who had written poetry expressing their thoughts about the military oppression. The 'Blue Heaven' became too great a risk, and in order to protect the children, the doors of this thriving business closed.

Each night, those under the roof of the orphanage met together and prayed for their country and their needs, leaving everything in God's capable hands. After all, the children had an advocate in Jesus, who once reminded his disciples that little ones have 'angels in heaven [who] always see the face of my Father'.[6] Knowing too that God inhabits the praises of his people,[7] their best weapon to keep the devil from inciting discouragement was to recite Bible verses and sing their favourite hymns and choruses. This shifted their focus and reminded them that God was well aware of their situation. Finding no better place to hide than under God's wings, they often read Psalm 91, which starts:

Whoever dwells in the shelter of the Most High
will rest in the shadow of the Almighty.
I will say of the LORD, 'He is my refuge and my fortress,
my God, in whom I trust.'

These difficult times affected Wingate deeply. Having been singled out, he recognized that the day would come when the legacy of this family would be under his roof. Like his hero John Wayne, he wanted to save the day. He dreamt of finding a lucrative job that would provide the much-needed funds to care for children like himself who had found a safe home in the Daw Gyi and Daw Nge Orphanage.

Wingate began work assisting a man who drove a truck. They hauled garlic, chillies, onions and Shan tea to Tachileik on the border with Thailand, some 350 miles away. The trip took weeks, as the truck often broke down from mechanical failure, and during the rainy season, the dirt roads were rutted with pot-holes. To add to the challenge and danger, their route was patrolled by the government's Tatmadaw or rebel insurgents. In the span of a year, they made the trip three times. As his year's pay was 3,000 kyat, at the time less than £2,[8] the disillusioned young Wingate realized it was probably not worth the risk of coming into the crossfire of fighting forces.

Not one to give up easily, he then sought Burma's natural resources of rubies, amethyst and peridot gemstones in the mines at Mai Shu. Digging for rubies embedded in rocks was a gamble of squandering precious time. The little extracted from the mines was often taken by unscrupulous people or demanded by the military. Ending up empty-handed eight months later, he tried another mine in Mogok, but became disenchanted when all his work didn't expose a single precious gem.

Wingate's next job was even more of a financial flop. Each morning for six months, he and a friend hand shovelled sand into pick-up trucks for a construction company. Their pay of 5 to 15 kyat wasn't worth the effort in a day when a cup of coffee and a slice of bread cost 1 kyat. He finally secured a trucking job with reasonable pay. The money was a Godsend because he and his wife of six years were expecting again.

The process of gaining a wife had begun years earlier when he was just a teen. She had been introduced as Bella Noe. Living with her aunt because her parents were too poor to send her to school, she had visited the children's home to learn how to make Christmas decorations. When she left, the 15-year-old Wingate thought of her often. Her long, flowing black hair attracted his attention but, more importantly, she had an engaging sweet calm about her.

However, Bella, two-and-a-half years his junior, wasn't impressed. Upon returning to her home in Kayah State, she didn't think about the young, infatuated boy. His endearing countenance, which had won over the hearts of the aunts and sisters, was completely lost on her.

Five years later and undaunted, Wingate decided to pay a visit to Loikaw, home to the dark-haired girl he couldn't get out of his mind. Bella's mother and Emmerline had been good friends during the Japanese occupation, so he didn't arrive as a complete unknown. After seeing the serene-spirited girl again, he was certain she was the right one for him. The love-struck suitor set about chopping wood, cleaning or doing anything else that could win her parents' favour.

The measure of his success was apparent in the eyes of Bella's parents, but the undecided girl was still not persuaded. Convinced he was a man of character, her parents began pressuring their daughter to consider a future with Emmerline's adopted son. When it came time for Wingate to return home, he went away a little cheerier to Taunggyi, certain that he could find a way into Bella's heart.

The next trip back to Loikaw, Emmerline came along for support. Bella's parents were delighted to welcome them into their home because by now they were sure Wingate was right for their daughter. The hopeful admirer explained to his would-be bride that he was poor and she would live a simple life if she were to become his wife. Respecting the wishes of her parents, though still uncertain of her decision, she finally accepted his proposal.

Bella couldn't have entered the orphanage at a more needed time. Adapting quickly to her new duties as a wife, she assisted Carmeline, Emmerline and Jacqueline in the duties of a very large orphanage. She was just the blessing the Daw Gyi and Daw Nge Orphanage needed – as we read in Proverbs 19:14, surely 'a prudent wife is from the LORD'.

11

God Works as the Orphanage Numbers Increase

Jesus said, 'Let the little children come to me, and do not hinder them, for the kingdom of heaven belongs to such as these.'

Matthew 19:14

One guarantee for Bella upon marrying Wingate was that her life would never be the same. After all, not every new bride has three mothers-in-law. Her life consisted of helping her new relatives with the work of the children's home and adapting to her role as Wingate's wife. Years later she dedicated herself to raising their sons, Kuku and Austin, and daughter, Aurora. When the only daughter-in-law of the benefactresses caught the vision of adoption, she and her husband would later take in two boys from the orphanage – Riki and Sai Hom Hpa. This would all add to the pressure of not just caring for his own family but the reality of the needs of the orphanage.

Even as Emmerline and her sisters welcomed Wingate and Bella's children, the births were either interspersed or followed by the deaths of Emmerline's brothers, Hla Than and Tha Aye, and cousin Andrew. Only their sister Beatrice was still living, in Yangon (which was the military junta's new name for Rangoon).

The three unmarried sisters continued to nurture every child who came within the walls of their home. In the minds of Emmerline, Carmeline and Jacqueline, no one ever found their way to the Daw Gyi Daw Nge Orphanage by accident, no matter how bizarre the circumstances that had brought them there. A beautiful infant girl they named Beauty was wrapped in fabric that someone had left hanging in a tree. An unimaginable story surrounded the arrival of another throw-away child.

A man in Toungoo was briskly walking by a garbage dump, sorting out the day's activities in his mind. For a brief moment, his eye caught the movement of a rice sack among the refuse. He concluded that to move such a large bag, it must have been a rat. The more the hurried traveller thought about it, though, the more something did not feel right. Reconsidering, he returned to investigate.

A twisted string wound around the neck of the sack; a tight knot made the mystery bag more difficult to open. When he did get the knot undone, the curious man peered inside. Shock overtook him, for he discovered inside a 2-year-old girl curled up awkwardly and completely naked. Severely handicapped, the child was unable to talk, walk or even move her arms well.

The foundling was very weak and in need of immediate attention. Not knowing what to do, the man took her to an orphanage in the same town. Assessing the child's needs, the director said the institution couldn't accept her due to its inability to address her severe handicaps. The concerned rescuer didn't give up, however, as he sought another option. He contacted a social welfare agency in the same city and was referred to an agency in Taunggyi. As they forwarded on the man's case, workers in charge knew where the little girl might have a home – at the Daw Gyi and Daw Nge Orphanage.

Emmerline and her siblings had no prior experience with the extreme needs of a disabled child, but they weren't about to turn away someone whom God had brought to their doorstep. The orphanage residents immediately set about caring for the abandoned girl, now named May Pu. They helped her feel welcomed and loved. The toddler joined in the best that she could and, at night, slept with the others on mats on the floor. Without an educational programme specifically designed for her needs, schooling was not a part of May Pu's growing up years. However, she tried to obey commands and help with the chores as the other children did.

Lacking the ability to articulate or enunciate words, May Pu's verbal communication remained a mix of unintelligible sounds. At the age of 18, the social welfare placed her in the Phayaphyu Disabled and Orphanage Home in Taunggyi to facilitate adequate intervention for her further development.

At times it was too late for help. A young mother had run off with another man, leaving a baby girl behind with her husband. The father – feeling inadequate to care for his little one – left her in the care of a friend. The friend, however, was indifferent to the baby's welfare, feeding her water rather than milk or another nutritious drink. When the father woke up to the reality that his daughter was not thriving, he quickly took her to the Daw Gyi Daw Nge Orphanage.

Emmerline and her sisters named her Baby because she was so tiny and frail. They gave her milk until they thought she was old enough to try porridge. Even the rice gruel didn't stay down in her weak stomach. Though they made every effort to save her life, the petite tot died six months later. Though hers was sad, the majority of the children's stories are happy.

Seven-month-old Chomden* and her 2-year-old twin sisters were abandoned by their mother after her husband, in a drunken stupor, had tried to kill her. The father – too addicted to alcohol to care – irresponsibly deserted the children in a farm field. Crying in unison, the trio's distressed voices alerted the ears of a close neighbour. Recognizing the urgency to find them a good home, he took the helpless girls to Carmeline, Emmerline and Jacqueline. For a while, the mother came to visit the girls as they grew, occasionally donating towards their keep. Three years later, however, she remarried and later gave birth to a son. With a different life, the new wife and mother never returned to the orphanage. The father, meanwhile, continued to live alone, eventually dying of health issues resulting from his addiction.

The three girls thrived in the environment of so many supportive caregivers, brothers and sisters. Upon reaching adulthood, one of the twins became a midwife while the other took up work in her aunt's shop. The younger sister, Chomden, stayed on at the children's home in Taunggyi, completing a five-year chemistry programme. Additionally, she is accomplished in playing the violin and uses her extra time to help Emmerline and Bella with the workload at the children's home.

Often the children came in pairs or groups, and at times the caregivers weren't adequately prepared for the surprise. Twin boys were born to a couple in Ho Pong. The father died first, and shortly afterwards the mother passed away. With no relatives living close by to raise the twins and since most of the neighbours were indigent, no one wanted the responsibility of two more mouths to feed.

The community elders wrapped the little ones in cloth and stood out at the road, offering them to any passer-by. But still no one offered to take them. Finally, two young women from Taunggyi came along on their way to Ho Pong for a visit. They noticed the wailing coming from the two swaddled babies in the men's arms.

Rather than continuing on their way, after listening to the woeful tale, the women compassionately returned to Taunggyi with the boys and took them to a Roman Catholic children's home. However, the home's Mother Superior explained that the orphans did not meet the home's criterion and turned them away.

By late afternoon – waifs in hand – the two women arrived at the home run by Emmerline and her sisters. Their arrival set off a flurry of activity. The bazaar would close soon, so they sent a helper racing at top speed to buy bottles and formula. In the meantime, the soiled and smelly babies were cautiously bathed, for by then they were too weak to even cry. Once fed and with bellies full, Emmerline carefully placed the precious newcomers in bed beside her where she could be attentive to their every move.

Raising twins – as anyone blessed with them knows – can be twice the challenge. When one baby cries, it is certain the other will follow. All the love and effort given this duo turned out to be a blessing. The boys grew up into handsome and caring young men. Hpone Min Pine (Sarver) is inclined towards studying physics, with engineering in mind. His brother, Min Myo Pine (Costa) – who likes maths – has been blessed with musical abilities and loves to sing and play the guitar.

It would be fair to say that a number of orphans dream of having their own home and a forever family. Yet, remarkably, two girls who were given a chance to have all that, surprised everybody.

In December 2004, a 9.1-strength earthquake struck off the coast of Sumatra, Indonesia, creating a tsunami that caused more than 200,000 deaths.[1] The quake was felt in Myanmar's delta region. In one village, Myat May and her sister, Lay, were aged 8 and 6 when their parents were caught off guard and died in the flooding. Soon after they arrived at the children's home in Taunggyi, a military officer requested permission to adopt the two – a once in a lifetime opportunity. Under the three sisters' careful scrutiny and discernment, the man was given permission and the new daughters-to-be left for Yangon. The officer's family gave the girls things that most orphans could only dream of – money, new clothes and the option of perusing a refrigerator when they were hungry. In spite of the affluence, he returned with the girls in tow only a year later. They were unhappy at his home and missed the camaraderie and life at the Daw Gyi and Daw Nge Orphanage.

Earlier that same year, 2004, Bella had come to a crisis in her life. The heavy workload and strain of caring for so many children had compromised her immunity. At first she suffered just a fever and cough, but after weeks of a constant hacking cough, it became difficult to breathe. After consultations with three different doctors, the young mother still had no diagnosis for her problem and no cure in sight. She wondered if she might lose her life . . . more importantly, she wondered if she was *ready* to die.

The thought occurred to Wingate's wife that she had never carefully examined her life. Had she done something to make the Creator angry and was she suffering the consequences? Did God see her as a significant person in the midst of this massively complex world? Could she really call him, '*Abba*, Father,'[2] as Jesus had prayed? Or did he abandon children too, as happened in her country? As a witness to the broken lives of children she served, Bella understood the inadequacies of human nature. The battles for power, prestige and self-promotion played a greater role in most people's lives rather than truly caring about the welfare of others. However, the animosity and indifference weren't only in others; the mirror was also on herself.

She had been taught that Jesus gave up his life for no other reason than to win people's hearts – the same attitude she saw in Carmeline, Emmerline and Jacqueline – but she became aware that she had never fully embraced a strong faith of her own. God's love in the end captured her heart just as decades earlier it had transformed the heart of the sisters' mother, Nan Yone. Bella handed her life over to God, and shortly after that, her debilitating ailment went away.

The increased numbers in the children's home saw God work on their behalf by bringing in generous donors – even from foreign countries. The faithful daughter-in-law busied herself sewing designer pillowcases, cushion covers, potholders, table-cloths and napkins to be sold to help pay the students' school fees. Wingate worked diligently at, among many other tasks, washing the children's school uniforms. To one of his sons, it seemed that Wingate was always washing clothes. To anyone who asked what his father did for a living, the boy would reply that he was a 'washer'.

In spite of the help of the younger generation, the orphan-age was greatly impacted in 2006. Carmeline was bedridden for a year and passed away at the age of 83. Many had been well-acquainted with the oldest sister of Emmerline. A graduate of Judson College, she had become a teacher actively involved in her congregation's Home Mission Society, the church's youth programme, Christian Endeavour, and the Young Men's Christian Association (YMCA). An accomplished pianist and violin-ist, she also served her church as choir director. Every Sunday found her accompanying the congregation on piano as Dr Bill Hackett led services at 4 in the afternoon. Not the least was her role in the incredibly challenging work of helping her family to care for the impoverished children throughout the years.

While adjusting to the death of this sibling, Emmerline had to face another loss in a little over a year.

One afternoon, Jacqueline had tutored a student until 4.30, then suddenly started to complain that she didn't feel well. Taken immediately to a hospital, she died by 10.30 that night. She was 69. Jacqueline had graduated from Rangoon University. She and Emmerline had both taught in the government schools until 1989. Even before she went to college, she had begun work as an English translator for a military attaché – a job she kept for thirty years.

An eloquent speaker, Jacqueline had often served as master of ceremonies and chairperson at important occasions and festivals. Like her father, Bani, she was active in Endeavour and enjoyed singing in the choir.

Through the years, Sein's children would sing double quartets. When some of the siblings passed away, their singing was reduced to one quartet. Eventually it became the trio of Carmeline, Jacqueline and Emmerline. Their songs had been a sound of sweet harmony to their listeners and a heartfelt demonstration of love for God.

Two daughters were the only remaining children of Bani and Nan Yone. Beatrice remained in Yangon, while Emmerline – at the age of 75 – became the sole overseer of almost 150 children who continued to come to the orphanage for the most heart-rending reasons.

12

Each with a Story of Their Own

*If anyone causes one of these little ones – those who be-
lieve in me – to stumble, it would be better for them if
a large millstone were hung round their neck and they
were thrown into the sea.*

Mark 9:42

Bennu* stopped playing long enough to watch an older woman
bend over to wash her colourful *longyi*. It was not unusual to
be in the company of neighbours since her mum had died over
three years ago. As long as the girl could remember, her family
had warned that fighting could come at any moment. But she
had no idea why. Grandmother's words were frightening as she
sternly cautioned her granddaughter that soldiers were known
to thrust children into the fire or throw them into the air and
plunge bayonets into their bodies. As these horrible thoughts
impressed her young mind, Bennu shuddered. It wasn't long
before the fearsome prediction became the child's reality.

A loud commotion alerted the small Karen community as
men barked out brutal orders. When the sound of gunfire
erupted, the terrified people ran in all directions. Smoke rising
to the sky announced the fires set by the soldiers that were con-
suming the dry grass and bamboo huts. At first paralysed by

terror, Bennu quickly recovered and intuitively ran towards the toilet. A man frantically scrutinized those running past him, looking for the familiar face of his daughter. But things were happening too fast. Now he had only two choices: run and save his own life or be shot in the ambush.

Wide-eyed, the terrified girl cowered in agonizing silence. She listened for footsteps amid the musty and toxic stench of the toilet. When the chaos had completely subsided, she cautiously opened the door. In the slaughter scene outside, bodies were strewn around the burnt village. But where was her father?

Three hours passed before she recognized the sound of her father shouting out her name. Crying, the 5-year-old sprinted in the direction of his call. Pure relief at running towards some sense of sanity engulfed her. But the naïve girl had no idea that in this disaster, her secure world had dissolved and now everything was about to change.

The raid's aftermath displaced many people, giving them no other choice but to leave their destroyed lives and find a new beginning. Bennu's father wanted her in a safer place; it couldn't be with him. Her aunt took her to a refugee camp on Myanmar's border with Thailand. Having lost his few worldly possessions, the destitute man, too, left in search of another life.

Separated from her only parent, the young evacuee went to live among thousands of other families in a landscape of small wooden houses. Schooling was organized by a non-governmental organization (NGO) – an education the Myanmar government refused to validate. Long and drawn out, each day offered little change and few opportunities. In addition to clothing and mosquito nets, the camp provided rice, vegetables and occasionally meat. Sometimes soldiers visited the encampment, awakening Bennu's nightmare all over again. As weeks turned into months and then years, the face of the only man she'd ever loved, her father, never appeared again. Nor did she hear him calling out her name as he had before. His concern for her was overridden by an obligation to his current wife and children. Additionally, he had been diagnosed with terminal lung cancer.

After six years of living among the refugees, Bennu was taken to Emmerline's orphanage by a concerned Christian woman. This sweet teenage girl did not allow her former life to imprison her with bitterness. Instead, God formed in her a generous and wise heart. She dreams of becoming a nurse.

The violent attack on this Karen girl's village was not one isolated infringement of human rights. Killing, raping, looting, destroying entire communities to force resettlement, kidnapping children and conscripting them to become porters or child soldiers are a few of the accusations thrown at the Tatmadaw, and at times the insurgent armies. But whether in uniform or not, what people have allowed to happen to the little ones God entrusts to them is not only deplorable, but inexcusable. A Lahu child[1] was only 4 years old when he saw his entire family killed by soldiers.

Another boy – from Nam Tee Village – was 3 when the military came to his small community of huts demanding that all the men become porters, including his father. On threat of losing their lives, they were forced to go with the army.

Only women were left to work in the fields as farmers. Now the young boy's mother was the sole provider for her two young sons and three older daughters. Every day the boy, Kywe,* and his family lived with the burden of insecurity adding to the pain of their poverty.

After four long and precarious years, the father escaped from the unjust enslavement and rejoined his family. This freedom was short-lived, however, as the government fighters returned and looted the Lahu people again – killing and raping as well as burning the huts and fields. With threats, and rifles shoved in their faces, a few boys were kidnapped and forced to be porters. Before they were harmed, Kywe's family fled to a mining community, Ke Ma Phyu.

The community had no school, so a year later, Kywe and his little brother were taken to Emmerline's orphanage. It seemed the most suitable place to live to receive an education. At times, this traumatized boy cries, thinking back on what his family endured. Recalling that his mother only visited him once, he is learning about the power of Christ's healing that comes through forgiveness. He talks of one day becoming an evangelist.

Boys in Myanmar – often as young as 10 years old – have been recruited and conscripted into the military and insurgent armies. Families attempt to evade this future for their sons by sending them off to live in monasteries or homes far from their villages. Over the years of civil war, reports have surfaced that juveniles were used to sweep for landmines; many others fell victims to sex trafficking. Different publications have documented this sobering reality; the Burmese army, however, denies such allegations.

Youngsters at risk have been brought to Emmerline's orphanage by concerned teachers, neighbours, relatives or Christians intervening on behalf of those neglected or abused. In some cases, the children are temporarily removed from their parents; other times it means permanent separation.

A Pa-O girl had one brother and five sisters. Her parents existed in extreme poverty in the Shan State like so many others suffering under years of military rule and socialism. The family's bamboo and thatch home was so tiny it barely housed the six children, forcing their parents to sleep outside under the stars in spite of the elements. Most of their days were spent securing food, and more often than not the children were hungry. Basic needs – like mosquito nets – were not even a consideration.

Shway* was certain, though, that her father loved her and she believed it with all her heart. His actions however, spoke otherwise. What small amount of money he earned often ended up in his pocket, rather than in his wife's purse on her way to the market. His taste for alcohol was addictive and, in his daughter's words, transformed him into a 'monster'. The alcoholic's drunkenness turned into violent behaviour towards his wife and children. As evidence of his abuse became more apparent, a receptive and caring teacher intervened. Deeply concerned for her student's welfare, she took the 6-year-old to the Daw Gyi and Daw Nge Orphanage for help.

The other children were taken to Yangon, and Shway never saw her siblings again. When the growing teen talks of this family of the past, her tears turn into inconsolable sobbing. The deep hurt wasn't inflicted by an unknown soldier; it came from the person she most loved and trusted. Despite the hurt, she has learned that Christ is dependable and if anyone is a part of God's family, it is forever.

With Myanmar's children, orphanages stand in the gap when parents will not or cannot offer their offspring adequate support. For instance, if the crops fail, the family budget can't handle the school fees and expenses. A large household might be forced to do a type of triage – deciding which son(s) or daughter(s) will live at an institution and which ones will remain in the home. Most ethnic groups in this predominantly Buddhist country believe strongly in education and are willing to sacrifice the unity of their family in order to provide what they believe is in the best interest of their child. Perhaps a relative may return to the orphanage with a little bit of money to help with support. Other households, however, live too far away and parents never return at all.

In one case, the parents of six dependants did not have access to clean water and they struggled to adequately provide sustenance for their children. Dividing their household into two groups, they kept the smallest ones and sent the older children to Emmerline's orphanage. Over the last four years, the third oldest child, San,* has learned with her two older sisters to depend upon each other. The girls have not seen their mother, father or younger siblings since leaving home.

Another child arrived at Emmerline's home at the age of 4. Korina grew up in an area where tungsten ore is mined and used in gunmetal. With loose environmental restrictions, the area's water becomes polluted. To prevent their daughter from developing health issues, the parents decided to relocate her to Taunggyi. Now aged 8, this Karen girl thinks she had three other siblings in her family. But since no one has ever come to visit her, she is not sure if that is true.

Other times, a divorced person, widow, or widower remarries, only to discover that their biological youngsters are not accepted into the new family. To preserve the new marriage, they desert their first brood. Sometimes grandparents attempt to raise the abandoned grandchildren. With few resources of their own, they too may give up.

A Karen boy's parents separated when he was just a year old. The grandmother took her grandson, Thet,* and in good faith tried to raise him by herself. After three years of caring for a young child, she was so fatigued that she gave him up to the Taunggyi orphanage. His mother remarried and moved on with her new life. The father remarried and produced two more children by his second wife. Contacting Emmerline, the man requested that his first son come to join his new family.

They were living in a refugee camp at the time, where he had applied for a US visa. The aged matriarch heard of it, however, and refused to grant her ex-son-in-law permission for fear the new stepmother would never treat Thet as her own.

Over the years, good Samaritans[2] have taken it upon themselves to bring the young ill-fated victims of war or poverty to the Daw Gyi Daw Nge Orphanage. They aren't afraid to travel on foot or ride motorcycles from as far away as 500 miles. When some of the refugee camps were closed down in 2016, Emmerline received thirty-two children in one day. They were dirty, hungry, without shoes and traumatized by what life had pressed upon them. The only possession they could call their own was a story to tell.

13

All in a Day's Work

And if anyone gives even a cup of cold water to one of these little ones who is my disciple, truly I tell you, that person will certainly not lose their reward.

Matthew 10:42

The soft-spoken woman shyly pulled her dark hair back, ignoring the loose wisps around her forehead. 'You have to learn to be humble,' she laughed, as she explained the difficulties growing up in the Daw Gyi and Daw Nge Orphanage. 'And it is important to love and respect everyone.' Her name is Cherry, and she came to the children's home at the age of 7 with her younger sister, from a village near Inle Lake. Her parents could not afford her educational expenses. 'It was very difficult at first learning how to get along [with the other children],' she confessed. But she did succeed, growing up to later complete a six-month training course to become a nurse's aide. She also became a wife and mother.

Another girl, Mya Zin, arrived at the Taunggyi institution at 4 years of age because there was no school in her small town. Twenty years later, she has a bachelor's degree in geography from Taunggyi University and has returned to the place of her birth to teach in a government school building.

The area's residents collect money for her salary. Mya Zin smiles as she testifies, 'I became a Christian at the age of 15. Now I share Christ with my family and all the other villagers.'

The bustling activity at the well-used, pastel teal-blue building begins early. The 88-year-old woman rises at 5.30 a.m. unless she has already been up at 1 or 2 a.m. to pray. She checks on the two women employees who are busy in the kitchen getting ready for the 7 a.m. breakfast. Today they will serve steamed rice and salt for the meal, although the children prefer fried rice with egg. An additional fifteen eggs would be required but, on this day, they don't have them available. This paddy grain is cooked in an old but reliable 5 ft metal steamer with five built-in shelves to hold the large, rounded aluminium pans. The early morning meal will be scooped out for almost a hundred hungry tummies.

Students of all ages put their mats away and dress in their numbered uniform for school – a cost of £5 to £13 each depending upon the size. For most of them, chores come before the morning sustenance. Eating beforehand are those who afterwards will squat to wash the dishes outside in three ground-level, light-weight metal tubs. The others comb out the hair of the younger ones, scrub floors, chop wood, or clean clothes in the only washer – a singularly divided machine. The left basin agitates the soapy water while the right basin spins the clothes enough to be hung outside to dry. The youngest workers are assigned to sweep floors or clean out the small exterior cement ditch that transports the water.

Burmese education runs from June to March, avoiding the intense heat of the tropical climate. The eager learners leave for morning classes as seven hired teachers arrive for the on-site preschool (begun while Gyi and Nge were still alive). Fifteen children come to this early childhood classroom. If their parents can afford to, they pay a fee for these services. About midday, lunch will be served for everyone. The hard-working scholars who have left the premises earlier in the day walk back from school for noon break.

Since rice is cooked for every meal, the orphanage uses an entire basket of this Asian staple daily. It is supplemented with curry, fish paste and vegetables, depending on the season. If affordable, once or twice a month meat is added for protein – fish, pork or chicken. The latter requires five birds, with each cut up into twenty-eight pieces. For special occasions, an elongated doughnut-type bread is fried in oil in large woks with lids over a heavy and rectangle-shaped cement wood-fired stove.

Emmerline's faith is strong, as she trusts that the children will be fed three times a day. Some years ago, when the cooks were down to a half bag of rice, a widow came asking for help. She had nothing to eat. Emmerline gave out of their poverty the last of the pantry, much to her sisters' chagrin. That very night a friend dropped by to donate a new sack, which doubled what had been given away.

More recently, another wife with four children came to the home in need of food and left the premises with supplies. The next day, a donor brought by ten bags of rice, salt, four tins of oil and 300 eggs. The wise Emmerline knew she could not out-give God.

As the day starts to ebb, the afterschool activities find the younger kids at play in the small courtyard with donated toy cars, colouring books or playing hide-and-seek, hitting a ball with a stick, tossing marbles, competing in a form of hop-scotch, and just chasing each other around. The older set continue on with their studies.

Due to Myanmar's closure to the outside world for so many years, the quality of the education in schools dropped considerably. Many students attend tutoring programmes, which are relatively expensive. Hired educators – who are poorly paid – augment their current teacher salaries by offering subjects outside the classroom.

During the vacation months of March to May, creative activities are explored. If a donor gives extra funds or offers to teach music lessons, a budding performer can reap the benefit of expressing himself though the arts. Volunteers teach the Karen language or demonstrate the skill of traditional weaving. Would-be artists are encouraged to draw and paint to develop their talents. Bella and other volunteers teach the older girls the skills of sewing and embroidering, enabling the newly trained seamstresses to make phone bags, cushion covers, pillowcases, aprons and bedspreads.

Wingate, on the other hand, offers agricultural experience to the teens – both male and female – who work alongside him at a five-acre farm within ten miles of the orphanage. The farm was given and partially developed by The Hackett Mission Legacy[1] from the United States. A few boys stay at the farm to attend a nearby school. Others come out on holidays to help cultivate the crops. The dry season produces potatoes, corn and garlic, while the rainy season sees cauliflower and cabbage brought in. The farm also has room for thirty pigs, adding income or food for the orphanage's very extended table.

In the evening, after the last meal of the day, everyone gathers for family devotions. The faces of Maunggyi and Sein, Bani and Nan Yone, Ukanbu, the aunts, and Emmerline's brothers and sisters smile from faded colour or black-and-white framed portraits, set against blue paint on a roughly textured wall. Several rows of small golden trophies imprinted with an icon of a cross and Bible lie below the photo gallery, impressing an observer with the success of those who have blossomed in this place. Sweet voices sing hymns of old with phrases of timeless truths. Emmerline pushes her rounded spectacles up on her nose so she can clearly see the words that have sustained her though the years. 'Even though I walk through the darkest valley,' she begins, 'I will fear no evil . . .'[2]

After the Bible lesson is read, the children bow their heads and prayers are lifted up. This space of forty minutes is a special time of bonding and nurturing. As the evening wanes, the children head off to bed to sleep next to each other on mats on the floor. Never mindful of her age, the lady of the house usually doesn't settle in bed until 11 p.m. or midnight, sometimes with little sleepers right beside her. Come morning, the daily routine will start all over again.

Over the years, twenty ethnic groups have resided under the roof of this blessed sanctuary – the diversity representing the open hearts of this remarkable Karen family. As the orphans and underprivileged venture out on their own, some stay in Taunggyi, but others go to the larger Myanmar cities of Mandalay and Yangon, or to countries such as China and Thailand. Emmerline – Ms Emerald – is concerned for each child's welfare as they leave her nest.

Dangerous pitfalls threaten Myanmar's people, especially the nation's children. Child trafficking is an ever-present threat, and children are used in forced marriages, as porters, in the military and for slavery and sexual exploitation. The children are taught to be aware of their surroundings and stay in groups. If they go on with their education and develop practical vocational skills, they have a better chance of not falling prey to such evil. There are many heart-warming stories of the children who became doctors, military officers, mechanics, teachers and nurse's aides, to name a few of their vocations. Those who attend higher education pass entrance exams to do so and have been blessed with scholarships from generous donors and the Yangon YMCA.

Emmerline has been asked numerous times what motivated her to give her entire life to serve so many. She never hesitates to answer from the joy inside of her that springs up as a twinkle in her eyes and a smile on her face. Referring to her grandmother Sein, grandfather Maunggyi, and the uncle and aunts, she explains: 'This is the only way we can repay our benefactors and benefactresses for all that they did for us.' But if you crack open that answer and peek inside, over a thousand children are waving back at you. She truly loves each one.

The legacy given to her wasn't the work in the orphanage or it would have collapsed during the many hardships. Since real battles begin within the heart, and the most powerful weapon to defeat evil is love, their true heritage was passed down not from Sein but by God himself. This provided Emmerline's family with the strength to fight for the children in a country faced with much turmoil. It is the path in the valley that leads to true freedom.

Retirement is not in the plans for Emmerline. This spirited elderly woman vows to watch over the children until promoted to join the rest of the family who have gone before her, in heaven. She will continue to attempt great things and expect great things because she trusts in God. If a visitor listens carefully, they might overhear an ageing soloist quietly singing one of her favourite hymns in the hallways of the orphanage.

To love someone more dearly ev'ry day,
To help a wand'ring child to find his way,

To ponder o'er a noble tho't and pray,
And smile when evening falls,
And smile when evening falls,
This is my task.

To follow truth as blind men long for light,
To do my best from dawn of day till night,
To keep my heart fit for His holy sight,
And answer when He calls,
And answer when He calls,
This is my task.

And then my Savior by and by to meet,
When faith hath made her task on earth complete,
And lay my homage at the Master's feet,
Within the jasper walls,
Within the jasper walls,
This crowns my task.[3]

Epilogue

*But who am I, and who are my people, that we should
be able to give as generously as this? Everything comes
from you, and we have given you only what comes from
your hand.*

1 Chronicles 29:14

When Sein's family rescued children in the early part of the
twentieth century, they began using their own funds to provide
for the orphans. It wasn't until after 1988, when the family had
used every possible resource of their own, that major donors
came forward to help meet their needs.

The list of these benefactors would be too long to write out,
and no doubt one might be forgotten. In lieu of mentioning
any specific person's name, may satisfaction be found in the
tremendous good their gifts have done. May it be enough to
trust the truth expressed in Matthew 10:42 that God himself
will reward the charity given to these children.

On Daw Mya Shwe's death, the land and buildings of the
main orphanage site will be lost due to circumstances beyond
her control. Patrick Klein, with Vision Beyond Borders, has
begun raising funds to build a new compound for the Daw
Gyi Daw Nge Orphanage on the edge of Kalaw, a beautiful

hill town forty-four miles from Taunggyi and thirty-one miles from Inle Lake. At the proposed construction site, the air is clean and the view of rice fields, flora and verdant hills below is stunning. Besides two large dormitories and classrooms, a library and chapel are planned.

Instruction is planned in sewing, computing, woodwork, animal husbandry and organic cultivation, all within walking distance of the building site. Also operating as a boarding house, the orphanage will allow disadvantaged children to come to stay for YMCA camps to learn skills, and the gospel of Jesus Christ. A board of directors is already in place and will oversee the new site and eventual employees.

If you would like to donate towards this development or the purchase of any equipment, animals, seeds, or a variety of other needed items to kick-start the new location, please feel free to contact Vision Beyond Borders. You can also pray for the children and visit them on a short-term mission trip. Check for travel dates on VBB's website:

Vision Beyond Borders
PO Box 2635
Casper, WY 82602
International Calling: 001 307 333 6545 Casper, WY.
info@visionbeyondborders.org

Bibliography/resources

Burmese names do not have surnames, therefore will appear in the order of their complete name excluding any honorific.

'2004 Indian Ocean Tsunami: Facts, FAQs, and How to Help', World Vision, 2004, https://www.worldvision.org/disaster-relief-news-stories/2004-indian-ocean-tsunami-facts (accessed 7 August 2019).

Allen, Louis, *Burma: The Longest War 1941–45* (London: Phoenix Press, 1984).

Appleton, George, 'Project Canterbury: The War and After: Burma' (London: The Society for the Propagation of the Gospel, c. 1946), http://anglicanhistory.org/asia/burma/appleton 1946/ (accessed 6 August 2019).

Arnold, Katy, 'Myanmar's poor crippled by debt to loan sharks', August 2018, https://www.axios.com/myanmar-child-labor-loan-sharks-debt-cea775da-e542-4625-b331-c31f76c57eec.html (accessed 29 July 2019).

Aung-Thwin, Michael & Maitrii Aung-Thwin, *A History of Myanmar Since Ancient Times: Traditions and Transformations* (London: Reaktion Books, 2012).

Aye Nyein Win, 'Looking back: education in the 1960s', *Myanmar Times*, May 2013, https://www.mmtimes.com/special-features/165-back-to-school-2013/6759-back-in-my-day-education-in-the-1960s.html (accessed 13 July 2019).

'Baptist Missionaries at Work in 19th-Century Burma', Connecticut History.org, https://connecticuthistory.org/spreading-love-and-hope-halfway-around-the-19th-century-world/ (accessed 30 July 2019).

Bella, personal interview, March–April 2018 to April 2019.

'Buddhism: The Four Noble Truths', BBC – Religions 2009, (web), https://www.bbc.co.uk/religion/religions/buddhism/beliefs/fournobletruths_1.shtml (accessed 12 May 2019).

'Burma's Ethnic Minorities', Canadian Friends of Burma, www.cfob.org/ethnicgroups-2/ (accessed 7 August 2019).

'Burma Independence Army', *Encyclopaedia Britannica* (2019), https://www.britannica.com/biography/Aung-San (accessed 6 August 2019).

Cheprasov, Artem, 'The Karen People: Culture & History', Study.com, https://study.com/academy/lesson/the-karen-people-culture-history.html (accessed 29 July 2019).

EveryStudent.com, 2000, https://www.everystudent.com/features/bible.html (accessed 5 August 2019).

Dhammananda Maha Thera, Venerable K. Sri, 'What Buddhists Believe', BuddhaSusana, A Buddhist Page by Binh Anson, 2011, https://www.budsas.org/ebud/whatbudbeliev/209.htm (accessed 12 May 2019).

'FAQs on Buddhist Culture', Buddhist Studies: Buddha Dharma Education Association & BuddhaNet (2008), https://www.buddhanet.net/e-learning/history/b_faqs.htm (accessed 12 May 2019).

Faure, Bernard, 'The Myth of the Historical Buddha', *Tricycle* magazine, Spring 2016, https://tricycle.org/magazine/myth-historical-buddha/ (accessed 12 May 2019).

Fong, Jack, *Revolution as Development: The Karen Self-Determination Struggle Against Ethnocracy (1949–2004)* (Boca Raton, FL: Universal Publishers 2008).

Gupte, Prajakta 'Child Soldiers in Myanmar: Role of Myanmar Government and Limitations of International Law', 6 Penn. St. J.L. & Int'l Aff. 2018, https://elibrary.law.psu.edu/jlia/vol6/iss1/15 (accessed 29 July 2019).

Hayami, Yoko, 'Karen Culture of Evangelism and Early Baptist Mission in Nineteenth Century Burma', *Brill*, August 2018, volume 31: issue 3–4, https://brill.com/view/journals/ssm/31/3-4/article-p251_3.xml?lang=en (accessed 29 July 2019).

Haydena, Martin & Richard Martin, 2013, 'Recovery of the Education System in Myanmar', *Journal of International and Comparative Education*, volume 2: issue 2, pp. 47–57, October 2013, https://www.researchgate.net/publication/291215887_Recovery_of_the_Education_System_in_Myanmar (accessed 13 July 2019).

Hays, Jeffrey, 'Education in Myanmar', May 2014, http://factsanddetails.com/southeast-asia/Myanmar/sub5_5f/entry-3117.html (accessed 14 July 2019).

—'British Rule of Burma', 14 May 2014, http://factsanddetails.com/southeast-asia/Myanmar/sub5_5a/entry-3007.html (accessed 3 August 2019).

—'Karen Ethnic Group', May 2019, http://factsanddetails.com/asian/cat66/sub417/entry-3935.html (accessed 29 July 2019).

—'Ne Win Years in Burma in the 1960s, 70s and 80s', May 2014, http://factsanddetails.com/southeast-asia/Myanmar/sub5_5a/entry-3010.html (accessed 29 July 2019).

—'People, Population, Languages of Myanmar', May 2014 http://factsanddetails.com/southeast-asia/Myanmar/sub5_5c/entry-3032.html (accessed 3 August 2019).

Hla Shwe, Daw (Beatrice), March–April 2018, April 2019.

Howard, Randolph L., *Baptists in Burma* (Philadelphia, PA: Judson Press, 1931).

Hull, Brian, 'Diffusion of Christian Endeavor', Paper Presentation at the Association of Youth Ministry Educators, October 2014, https://www.aymeducators.org/wp-content/uploads/Diffusion-of-Christian-Endeavor-Hull.pdf (accessed 30 April 2020).

Jolliffe, Kim, 'Ceasefires, Governance, and Development: The Karen National Union in Times of Change', December 2016, https://asiafoundation.org/wp-content/uploads/2017/02/Ceasefires-Governance-and-Development-EN-Apr2017.pdf (accessed 13 July 2019).

Kapi, Saw, 'Revolution Reviewed: The Karen's Struggle for Right to Self-determination and Hope for the Future', Unconventional Thoughts & Commentaries, February 2006, https://ieds.blogspot.com/2006/02/revolution-reviewed.html (accessed 6 August 2019).

'Karen', *Encyclopedia of World Cultures*, copyright 2020. The Gale Group, Inc., https://encyclopedia.com/places/asia/south-asia-physical-geography/karen (accessed 28 April 2020).

'Karen History', Karen Organization of Minnesota, https://www.mnkaren.org/history-culture/karen-history/ (accessed 30 July 2019).

'Longest Wars in Human History', World Facts: World Atlas, 2019, (web), https://worldatlas.com/articles/longest-wars-in-human-history.html (accessed 7 August 2019).

Lyte, Henry Francis (1793–1847), 'Abide with Me', Public Domain, https://www.youtube.com/watch?v=58ZxNVIuXFw (accessed 3 September 2019).

Loo-Nee, Sandra, telephone interview, April 2018 to August 2019.

Maung Aung Myoe, *Building the Tatmadaw: Myanmar Armed Forces Since 1948* (Singapore: Institute of Southeast Asian Studies, 2009).

'Mongnai–Myanmar (Burma)', map, Google. tinyurl.com/y57nfg4j.

Myanmar casinos and gambling guide. World Casino Directory (accessed 29 July 2019). https://www.worldcasinodirectory.com/myanmar (accessed 30 July 2019).

'Myanmar: Tatmadaw leaders must be investigated for genocide, crimes against humanity, war crimes', UN report, 27 August 2018, https://www.ohchr.org/EN/HRBodies/HRC/Pages/NewsDetail.aspx?NewsID=23475&LangID=E (accessed 13 July 2019).

Mya Shwe, Daw (Emmerline), December 2017, March–April, December 2018, April 2019.

Naw Say Pwe, 'The Beginning of Karen Education in Irrawaddy Division During the British Colonial Period', 2018, https://www.academia.edu/38154051/The_Beginning_of_Karen_Education_in_Irrawaddy_Division_During_the_British_Colonial_Period (accessed 30 July 2019).

Oxford Burma Alliance, 'The Ne Win Years: 1962–1988', http://www.oxfordburmaalliance.org/1962-coup-ne-win-regime.html (accessed 7 August 2019).

Partridge, Rhianon, Wah Wah Naw, Daniel Zu, Lina Ishu, Gary Cachia with additional input provided by Jasmina

Bajraktarevic Hayward, 'STARTTS Karen Community Consultation report', 28 March 2009, p. 4, https://www.startts .org.au/media/Karen-Community-Consultation-Report-final-09.pdf (accessed 30 July 2019).

Pau, Cope Suan, 'Interpreting Religious Conversions among the Peoples of Myanmar: Assimilating the Christian Faith into the Local Cultural Heritages and the Impact of Christian Mission during the Colonial Era' (2013), A Doctor's Dissertation, Doctor of Theology in Mission Studies, https://nikonghong.files.wordpress.com/2013/01/dissertation.pdf (accessed 30 July 2019).

Phone (pseudonym for a disabled child cared for at the orphanage), personal interview, April 2018.

Pramanik, Dr. B. K., 'Christian Endeavor in Asia', A Brief History of Christian Endeavor, http://www.worldsceunion .org/files/CE-Asia.pdf (accessed 12 May 2020).

Ray, Maude Louise (1880–?), 'To Love Someone More Dearly', Public Domain, https://www.youtube.com/watch?v=HJe6fL RF5VA (accessed 4 September 2019).

Read, Katherine L. with Robert O. Ballou, *Bamboo Hospital* (Philadelphia, PA: J.B. Lippincott Company, 1961).

Richardson, Don, *Eternity in Their Hearts* (Bloomington, MN: Bethany House Publishers, a division of Baker Publishing Group, 2006; 1st edn, 1984).

'Rohingya not only group persecuted in Myanmar, Christian minorities are as well', AsiaNews.it. 3 October 2017, http://www .asianews.it/news-en/Rohingya-not-only-group-persecuted-in-Myanmar,-Christian-minorities-are-as-well-41952.html (accessed 29 July 2019).

Sai Htwe Maung, *History of Shan Churches in Burma (Myanmar)*, 2007, pp. 32-104, https://www.yumpu.com/en/

document/read/23824853/history-of-shan-churches-in-burma-1861-2001-khamkoo (accessed 12 May 2020).

Sao Sanda Yawnghwe Simms, *The Moon Princess: Memories of the Shan States* (Bangkok: River Books, 2008).

SarDesai, D.R., *Southeast Asia Past and Present* (Boulder, CO: Westview Press, 2013).

Sargent, Inge, *Twilight Over Burma: My Life as a Shan Princess* (Honolulu: University of Hawaii Press, 1994).

'Should It Be Burma or Myanmar?' BBC News Magazine 2007, http://news.bbc.co.uk/2/hi/7013943.stm (accessed 7 August 2019).

Taylor, Robert H., General Ne Win: A Political Biography (Singapore: ISEAS Publishing, 2015).

Thanakha Team, 'Burma Women's Voices for Hope', Bangkok, May 2007, https://www.peacewomen.org/sites/default/files/hr_part_burmawomenvoicesforhope__altseanburma_2007_0.pdf (accessed 14 July 2019).

Tha Nyan, Dr, personal interview, December 2017, March–April 2018, April 2019.

The Baptist Missionary Magazine, volumes 59–60, American Baptist Missionary Union (Boston, MA: 1879), preview .tinyurl.com/y566h5a8 (accessed 29 July 2019).

'The Colonial Era (1885–1948)', Harvard Divinity School, Religious Literacy Project, 2019, https://rlp.hds.harvard.edu/for-educators/country-profiles/myanmar/colonial-era-1885-1948 (accessed 14 August 2019).

'The Glory of Christ: 5 Ways Jesus Proved He Was the Messiah', Billy Graham Evangelistic Association, 24 December 2015, https://billygraham.org/story/the-glory-of-christ-5-ways-jesus-proved-hes-the-messiah/ (accessed 5 August 2019).

'The Hackett Mission Legacy: Honoring over 100 years of service in Burma since 1913', https://thehackettmissionlegacy .org (accessed 29 July 2019).

'The Indian National Army, 1942–1945', Historynet, https:// www.historynet.com/indian-national-army1942-45 .htm (accessed 6 August 2019).

'The Japanese Occupation', the Museum of Karen History and Culture, 2005, https://burmalibrary.org/docs3/ karenmuseum-01/History/japanese_occupation.htm#_ftn3 (accessed 13 July 2019).

'The Origins of Buddhism', Asia Society, Center for Global Education, 2018, https://asiasociety.org/education/origins-buddhism(accessed 12 May 2019).

Thirty children, teens and adults of the Daw Gyi Daw Nge Orphanage, personal interviews, 2017–19.

Tucker, Shelby, *Burma: The Curse of Independence* (London: Pluto Press, 2001).

'UN List of Least Developed Countries'. United Nations Conference on Trade and Development, https://unctad .org/en/pages/aldc/Least%20Developed%20Countries/UN-list-of-Least-Developed-Countries.aspx (accessed 7 August 2019).

Wingate, personal interview, March–April 2018.

World Directory of Minorities and Indigenous Peoples, 2019, Minority Rights Group International, https://minorityrights. org/country/myanmarburma/ (accessed 29 July 2019).

Zam Khat Kham, 'Burmese Nationalism and Christianity in Myanmar: Christian Identity and Witness in Myanmar Today', 2016, Doctor of Philosophy Dissertation, 22, Concordia (web), https://scholar.csl.edu/cgi/viewcontent .cgi?article=1021&context=phd (accessed 5 August 2019).

Notes

Preface

[1] An ankle-length cloth worn by both sexes, wrapped and tied in a knot around the waist.

[2] Jeffrey Hays, 'People, Population, Languages of Myanmar', 2008–2019, http://factsanddetails.com/southeast-asia/Myanmar/sub5_5c/entry-3032.html (accessed 3 August 2019). Also see 'World Directory of Minorities and Indigenous Peoples', 2019, Minority Rights Group International, https://minorityrights.org/country/myanmarburma/ (accessed 29 July 2019).

[3] See Psalm 23.

[4] Department of Social Welfare and UNICEF, 'The Situation of Children in Residential Facilities in Myanmar', August 2011, pp. 28–31.

1 God's Protection in Taunggyi

[1] The currency of Myanmar.

[2] See Romans 5:3–4.

2 Beginnings in the Irrawaddy Delta

1   D.R. SarDesai, *Southeast Asia Past and Present* (Boulder, CO: Westview Press, 2013), p. 11.
2   Renamed Ayeyarwady Delta in 1989.
3   Jeffrey Hays, 'People, Population, Languages of Myanmar', 2008–2019, http://factsanddetails.com/southeast-asia/Myanmar/sub5_5c/entry-3032.html (accessed 3 August 2019).
4   Karen Organization of Minnesota, 'Karen History,' 2017, https://www.mnkaren.org/history-culture/karen-history/ (accessed 16 May 2019).
5   Jeffrey Hays, 'British Rule of Burma', 2008–2019, http://factsanddetails.com/southeast-asia/Myanmar/sub5_5a/entry-3007.html#chapter-2 (accessed 3 August 2019).
6   Harvard Divinity School, Religious Literacy Project, 'The Colonial Era (1885–1948),' 2019, https://rlp.hds.harvard.edu/for-educators/country-profiles/myanmar/colonial-era-1885-1948 (accessed 14 August 2019).
7   Don Richardson, *Eternity in Their Hearts* (Bloomington, MN: Bethany House Publishers, 2006), pp. 66–77. Also see Cope Suan Pau, 'Interpreting Religious Conversions among the Peoples of Myanmar: Assimilating the Christian Faith into the Local Cultural Heritages and the Impact of Christian Mission during the Colonial Era', 2013, A Doctor's Dissertation, Doctor of Theology in Mission Studies, https://nikonghong.files.wordpress.com/2013/01/dissertation.pdf, 146–152 (accessed 30 July 2019). Also see Naw Say Say Pwe, 'The Beginning of Karen Education in Irrawaddy Division During the British Colonial Period', 2018, https://www.academia.edu/38154051/The_Beginning_of_Karen_Education_in_Irrawaddy_Division_During_the_British_Colonial_Period (accessed 30 July 2019).
8   Yoko Hayami, 'Karen Culture of Evangelism and Early Baptist Mission in Nineteenth Century Burma', *Brill*, August 2018, volume 31: issue 3–4, https://brill.com/view/journals/ssm/31/3-4/article-p251_3.xml?lang=en (accessed 29 July 2019).

9   Zam Khat Kham, 'Burmese Nationalism and Christianity in Myanmar: Christian Identity and Witness in Myanmar Today', 2016, Doctor of Philosophy Dissertation, 22, Concordia, https://scholar.csl.edu/cgi/viewcontent.cgi?article=1021&context=phd (accessed 5 August 2019).

10 Renamed Thanlwin in 1989.

11 Renamed Pathein in 1989.

12 Naw Say Say Pwe, 'The Beginning of Karen Education in Irrawaddy Division During the British Colonial Period', 2018, p. 227, https://www.academia.edu/38154051/The_Beginning_of_Karen_Education_in_Irrawaddy_Division_During_the_British_Colonial_Period (accessed 30 July 2019).

13 Renamed Mawlamyine in 1989.

14 Jeffrey Hays, 'British Rule of Burma', 2008–2019, http://factsanddetails.com/southeast-asia/Myanmar/sub5_5a/entry-3007.html (accessed 3 August 2019).

3 A Christian Family Among Buddhists

1   Billy Graham Evangelistic Association, 'The Glory of Christ: 5 Ways Jesus Proved He Was the Messiah', 24 December 2015, https://billygraham.org/story/the-glory-of-christ-5-ways-jesus-proved-hes-the-messiah/ (accessed 5 August 2019). Also see EveryStudent.com, 2000, https://www.everystudent.com/features/bible.html (accessed 5 August 2019).

2   Bernard Faure, *Tricycle* magazine, 'The Myth of the Historical Buddha', Spring 2016, https://tricycle.org/magazine/myth-historical-buddha/ (accessed 12 May 2019).

3   BBC – Religions – Buddhism: 'The Four Noble Truths', 17 November 2009, https://www.bbc.co.uk/religion/religions/buddhism/beliefs/fournobletruths_1.shtml (accessed 12 May 2019). Also see Asia Society, Center for Global Education, 'The Origins of Buddhism', 2018, https://asiasociety.org/education/origins-buddhism (accessed 12 May 2019).

4   Venerable K. Sri Dhammananda Maha Thera, 'What Buddhists Believe', BuddhaSusana, A Buddhist Page by Binh Anson, 2011, https://www.budsas.org/ebud/whatbudbeliev/209.htm (accessed 12 May 2019).

5   'For all have sinned and fall short of the glory of God' (Rom. 3:23).

6   'For the wages of sin is death, but the gift of God is eternal life in Christ Jesus our Lord' (Rom. 6:23).

7   'For God so loved the world that he gave his one and only Son, that whoever believes in him shall not perish but have eternal life' (John 3:16).

8   Venerable K. Sri Dhammananda Maha Thera, 'What Buddhists Believe', 2011, https://www.budsas.org/ebud/whatbudbeliev/209.htm (accessed 12 May 2019). Also see BuddhaSusana, A Buddhist Page by Binh Anson, https://www.burmalibrary.org/en/buddhasasana-a-buddhist-page-by-binh-anson, Buddhist Studies: Buddha Dharma Education Association & BuddhaNet, 'FAQs on Buddhist Culture', 2008, https://www.buddhanet.net/e-learning/history/b_faqs.htm (accessed 12 May 2019).

9   Venerable K. Sri Dhammananda Maha Thera, 'What Buddhists Believe', 2011, https://www.budsas.org/ebud/whatbudbeliev/209.htm (accessed 12 May 2019).

10 'He will punish those who do not know God and do not obey the gospel of our Lord Jesus. They will be punished with everlasting destruction and shut out from the presence of the Lord and from the glory of his might' (2 Thess. 1:8,9).

11 Sai Htwe Maung, *History of Shan Churches in Burma (Myanmar)*, 2007, p. 49, https://www.yumpu.com/en/document/read/23824853/history-of-shan-churches-in-burma-1861-2001-khamkoo (accessed 12 May 2020).

4 The Children and Grandchildren of Sein

1   A Christian non-denominational youth programme that originated in the United States in 1881 to promote Christian service,

discipleship and witnessing among the youth, under the leadership of the local churches. It was established as 'The Karen Baptist Christian Endeavour Union' in Burma in 1897. See Brian Hull, PhD, 'Diffusion of Christian Endeavor', Paper Presentation at the Association of Youth Ministry Educators, October 2014, https://www.aymeducators.org/wp-content/uploads/Diffusion-of-Christian-Endeavor-Hull.pdf (accessed 30 April 2020). Also see Dr. B. K. Pramanik, A Brief History of Christian Endeavor, 'Christian Endeavor in Asia', http://www.worldsceunion.org/files/CE-Asia.pdf (accessed 12 May 2020).

2   Matthew 10:42.

3   Henry Francis Lyte (1793–1847), 'Abide with Me', Public Domain, https://www.youtube.com/watch?v=58ZxNVIuXFw (accessed 3 September 2019).

6 Finding Refuge in the Japanese Occupation

1   The Hackett Mission Legacy: Honoring over 100 years of service in Burma since 1913, https://thehackettmissionlegacy.org/?page_id=15 (accessed 29 July 2019).

2   Read, Katherine L., with Robert O. Ballou, *Bamboo Hospital* (Philadelphia, PA: J.B. Lippincott Company, 1961), p. 198.

3   Encyclopaedia Britannica, 'Burma Independence Army', 2019, https://www.britannica.com/biography/Aung-San (accessed 6 August 2019).

4   'The Indian National Army, 1942–1945', Historynet, https://www.historynet.com/indian-national-army1942-45.htm (accessed 6 August 2019).

5   'The Japanese Occupation', The Museum of Karen History and Culture, 2005, http://burmalibrary.org/docs3/karenmuseum-01/History/japanese_occupation.htm#_ftn3 (accessed 13 July 2019).

6   George Appleton, Archdeacon of Rangoon, 'Project Canterbury: The War and After: Burma' (London: The Society for the Propagation of the Gospel, c. 1946), http://anglicanhistory.org/asia/burma/appleton1946/ (accessed 6 August 2019).

7 At War's End Emmerline Becomes a Woman

1 John 3:1–8.
2 2 Corinthians 6:14.
3 Romans 14:12.
4 Saw Kapi, 'Revolution Reviewed: The Karen's Struggle for Right to Self-determination and Hope for the Future', Unconventional Thoughts & Commentaries, February 2006, https://ieds.blogspot .com/2006/02/revolution-reviewed.html (accessed 6 August 2019).

8 The Family Flees Further Violence

1 'Longest Wars in Human History', World Facts: World Atlas, 2019, (web), www.worldatlas.com/articles/longest-wars-in-human-history.html (accessed 7 August 2019).
2 Artem Cheprasov, 'The Karen People: Culture & History', Study .com, https://study.com/academy/lesson/the-karen-people-culture-history.html (accessed 29 July 2019).
3 John 3:16.
4 John 4:1–42.

9 The Daw Gyi Daw Nge Orphanage and Old People's Home

1 Robert H. Taylor, *General Ne Win: A Political Biography* (Singapore: ISEAS Publishing, 2015), p. 255.
2 Maung Aung Myoe, *Building the Tatmadaw: Myanmar Armed Forces Since 1948* (Singapore: Institute of Southeast Studies, 2009), pp. 4, 19.
3 Taylor, *General Ne Win: A Political Biography*, op. cit., pp. 261–262.
4 Michael A. Aung-Thwin, Maitrii Aung-Thwin, *A History of Myanmar Since Ancient Times: Traditions and Transformations* (London: Reaktion Books, 2012), p. 247.

5   'UN List of Least Developed Countries'. United Nations Conference on Trade and Development, unctad.org/en/pages/aldc/Least%20 Developed%20Countries/UN-list-of-Least-Developed-Countries .aspx (accessed 7 August 2019). Also see Martin Haydena & Richard Martin, 'Recovery of the Education System in Myanmar,' *Journal of International and Comparative Education*, October 2013, https:// www.researchgate.net/publication/291215887_Recovery_of_the_ Education_System_in_Myanmar (accessed 13 July 2019). Also Jeffrey Hays, 'British Rule of Burma', 2008–2019, http://factsanddetails .com/southeast-asia/Myanmar/sub5_5a/entry-3007.html#chapter-2 (accessed 3 August 2019).

6   Jeffrey Hays, 'British Rule of Burma', 2008–2019, http:// factsanddetails.com/southeast-asia/Myanmar/sub5_5f/entry- 3117.html (accessed 3 August 2019).

7   Canadian Friends of Burma, 'Burma's Ethnic Minorities', http:// www.cfob.org/ethnicgroups-2/ (accessed 7 August 2019).

10 Wingate, the Only Adopted Child

1   Romans 3:23.

2   Source unknown.

3   Oxford Burma Alliance, 'The Ne Win Years: 1962–1988', http:// www.oxfordburmaalliance.org/1962-coup-ne-win-regime.html (accessed 7 August 2019). Also see Shelby Tucker, *The Curse of Independence* (London: Pluto Press, 2001), p. 228.

4   Oxford Burma Alliance, 'The Ne Win Years: 1962–1988', http:// www.oxfordburmaalliance.org/1988-uprising-1990-elections .html (accessed 7 August 2019).

5   BBC News Magazine, 'Should It Be Burma or Myanmar?' 2007, http://news.bbc.co.uk/2/hi/7013943.stm (accessed 7 August 2019).

6   Matthew 18:10.

7   Psalm 22:3.

8   Currency rate 1989 https://fxrate.net/historical/?c_input= MMK&cp_input=GBP&date_to_input=1989-04-28&range_ input=30 (accessed 28 April 2020).

11 God Works as the Orphanage Numbers Increase

1 World Vision, '2004 Indian Ocean Tsunami: Facts, FAQs, and How to Help', 2004, https://www.worldvision.org/disaster-relief-news-stories/2004-indian-ocean-tsunami-facts (accessed 7 August 2019).
2 Mark 14:36.

12 Each with a Story of Their Own

1 A minority tribe that lives on the border of Myanmar and Thailand.
2 See Luke 10:25–37.

13 All in a Day's Work

1 The Hackett Mission Legacy: Honoring over 100 years of service in Burma since 1913, https://thehackettmissionlegacy.org/?page_id=15 (accessed 29 July 2019).
2 Psalm 23:4.
3 Maude Louise Ray (1880–?), 'To Love Someone More Dearly', Public Domain, www.youtube.com/watch?v=HJe6fLRF5VA (accessed 4 September 2019).

Blood, Sweat and Jesus

The story of a Christian hospital bringing hope and healing in a Muslim community

Kerry Stillman

What is a Christian hospital doing in a remote Muslim area of Cameroon?

Kerry Stillman shares her own experiences of working as a physiotherapist in a sub-saharan village hospital. A vivid impression of daily life is painted as the team deal with the threat of terrorism, the attitudes of local people towards Western medicine, their patients' health issues, and the challenge of sensitively sharing the gospel in a different culture.

Passionate, intriguing and uplifting, this is a colourful interweaving of cultures, beliefs and the power of prayer alongside modern medicine.

978-1-78893-148-9

A Beautiful Tapestry

*Two ordinary women,
one amazing God,
many lives transformed*

*Tracy Williamson
with Marilyn Baker*

Being blind, Marilyn's childhood was one of increasing isolation whilst Tracy's was marked by deafness and low self-esteem. Yet from these most unlikely of origins, God brought these two remarkable ladies together in the most hilarious fashion and gave them a joint vision to work together through Marilyn Baker Ministries.

Through their work in prisons, concerts, retreats, conferences and prayer ministry, they have seen many lives transformed by the power of God's love. Many of those testimonies are included in this book, showing that God is indeed weaving a beautiful tapestry in all our lives. Each individual strand of yarn isn't much in itself, but when woven together an amazing picture emerges as he uses us in our weakness to show the beauty of his love to others.

978-1-78893-156-4

Ever Present

*Running to survive, thrive
and believe*

Austen Hardwick

Strokes, brain surgery, epilepsy . . . where is God in the middle of
our suffering?

After surviving three strokes in his forties, Austen Hardwick
began to think more deeply about life and faith. As he started to
recover, he realised that running created space in which he could
draw closer to God.

Weaving together personal testimony and biblical teaching,
Austen encourages us to run towards God rather than away from
him, so that we, too, can learn to live life in all its fullness with an
ever-present God who is with us in our struggles.

Genuine, real, and inspirational, *Ever Present* explores how
running can be good for both the heart and the soul.

978-1-78893-136-6

Salt Water and Honey

*Lost dreams, good grief,
and a better story*

Lizzie Lowrie

Reeling from the disappointment of a failed business venture, Lizzie Lowrie's life takes a nightmarish turn as she suffers miscarriage after miscarriage.

Written from the messy middle of life, where there are no neat or clichéd answers, Lizzie honestly shares her pain and the fight to find God in her suffering.

Providing a safe space to remind people that they're not alone, it's okay to grieve and their story matters, this is for anyone who has lost their dream and is struggling to understand their purpose when life looks nothing like they hoped it would.

978-1-78893-095-6

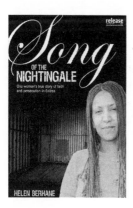

Song of the Nightingale

*One woman's true story of faith
and persecution in Eritrea*

Helen Berhane

Song of the Nightingale is the true story of Helen Berhane, held
captive for over two years in appalling conditions in her native
Eritrea. Her crime? Sharing her faith in Jesus, and refusing, even
though horrendously tortured, to deny him. A sobering, painful,
heart-rending account of true faith in the face of evil, this book
makes for uncomfortable and yet inspirational reading.

Helen says, 'I want to give a message to those of you who are
Christians and live in the free world: you must not take your freedom
for granted . . . If I could sing in prison, imagine what you can do for
God's glory with your freedom!'

A real challenge for the church in the West.

978-1-85078-864-5

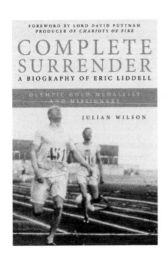

Complete Surrender

A Biography of Eric Liddell
Olympic Gold Medallist and Missionary

Julian Wilson

'On a stiflingly hot Parisian afternoon in July 1924, six athletes lined up for the start of the Olympic 400 metres. In the sixth and outside lane was the Scottish sprint sensation Eric Liddell . . .'

Liddell made headlines by refusing to race on a Sunday. His switch from 100 metres to 400 metres, and subsequent triumph, is now legendary.

Liddell brought the same singleness of purpose to his faith as to his running. This vivid biography recounts his career as a missionary in war-torn China, his unassuming and selfless character, and his delight in practical jokes. It includes interviews with his family and friends, extracts from his letters and a number of rare photographs.

978-1-86024-841-2

The Man in White

Extraordinary accounts of the
intervening power of
the living God

Dr Ernest F. Crocker

Many of us want to see Jesus, to hear his voice. We want a tangible experience of God.

As a Christian doctor and follower of Jesus, Ernest Crocker has been a witness to many interventions of God during his life. In *The Man in White*, he brings together an inspiring selection of testimonies from around the world of people who have seen God do extraordinary things in and through their lives. They include professionals, academics, a train robber, a surgeon facing decapitation for his faith, and those who have escaped the ravages of war.

hese powerful stories inspire and challenge us to see that God is real and delights in being involved in our lives today.

978-1-78893-133-5

A Time to Hope

*365 Daily devotions from
Genesis to Revelation*

Naomi Reed

Many of us have favourite Bible verses that we draw comfort
from, but we don't always know their context or understand how
they fit into the main story arc of the Bible.

Tracing the big picture of God's story through the key themes and
events from Genesis to Revelation allows us to see the abundant
riches in God's Word. As you read the unfolding story day by
day, you can encounter God in all his glorious holiness and
faithfulness.

If you have ever struggled to read the Bible from cover to cover,
then this devotional will help you find a way in to God's big story
and help you fall in love with Jesus all over again.

978-1-78893-144-1

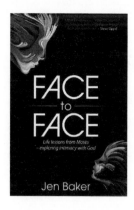

Face to Face

*Life lessons from Moses –
exploring intimacy with God*

Jen Baker

God longs for us to personally experience more of him, but so often we refuse or feel unable to draw close to him. Even the great hero of faith Moses hid his face from God, yet was eventually transformed into someone who spoke face to face with him.

Jen Baker explores Moses' life to see how he was able to move from hiddenness to holiness and encourages us to follow his example. Interwoven with personal testimony, Jen gently challenges and shows us how to move out of the shadows into the light of God's love.

Whether you feel distant from God or want to deepen your relationship with him, *Face to Face* will help encourage you to experience God in a new and powerful way.

978-1-78893-056-7

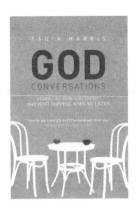

God Conversations

*Stories of how God speaks and
what happens when we listen*

Tania Harris

Stories of God talking to his people abound throughout the
Bible, but we usually only get the highlights. We read: 'God
said "Go to Egypt,"' and then, 'Mary and Joseph left for
Egypt.' We're not told how God spoke, how they knew it was
him, or how they decided to act on what they'd heard.

In *God Conversations*, international speaker and pastor Tania
Harris shares insights from her own story of learning to hear
God's voice. You'll get to eavesdrop on some contemporary
conversations with God in the light of his communication
with the ancients. Part memoir, part teaching, this unique and
creative collection will help you to recognize God's voice when
he speaks and what happens when you do.

978-1-78078-188-4

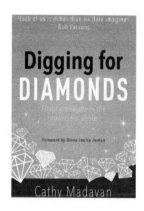

Digging for Diamonds

*Finding treasure in the
messiness of life*

Cathy Madavan

What is hidden always shapes what we can see. In this
book, Cathy Madavan encourages us to dig deeper and discover
more of the life-transforming treasures of our identity, strength,
character and purpose that God has already placed within us –
right where we are.

Cathy explores twelve key facets which point the reader to a
deeper understanding of their unique, God-given raw material
and how God wants to transform them to live a valuable,
purposeful life that will also unearth precious potential in others.

978-1-78078-131-0
Devotional: 978-1-78893-152-6

Finding Our Voice

*Unsung lives from the Bible
resonating with stories from today*

Jeannie Kendall

The Bible is full of stories of people facing issues that are still surprisingly relevant today. Within its pages, people have wrestled with problems such as living with depression, losing a child, overcoming shame, and searching for meaning. Yet these are not always the stories of the well-known heroes of faith, but those of people whose names are not even recorded.

Jeannie Kendall brings these unnamed people to vibrant life. Their experiences are then mirrored by a relevant testimony from someone dealing with a similar situation today.

Finding Our Voice masterfully connects the past with the present day, encouraging us to identify with the characters' stories, and giving us hope that, whatever the circumstances, we are all 'known to God'.

978-1-78893-037-6

A–Z of Prayer

*Building strong foundations for
daily conversations with God*

Matthew Porter

A–Z of Prayer is an accessible introduction that gives practical
guidance on how to develop a meaningful prayer life. It
presents twenty-six aspects of prayer to help you grow in your
relationship with God, explore new devotional styles and
deepen your daily conversations with God.

Each topic has a few pages of introduction and insight, an
action section for reflection and application and a prayer
to help put the action point into practice. There are also
references to allow further study.

978-1-78893-062-8

Authentic

We trust you enjoyed reading this book
from Authentic. If you want to be
informed of any new titles from this author
and other releases you can sign up to the
Authentic newsletter by scanning below:

Online:
authenticmedia.co.uk

Follow us: